the sermon
SUCKING BLACK HOLE

*the*SermoN
SUCKING
BLACK HOLE

Why You Can't Remember on Monday
What Your Minister Preached on Sunday

DAVID R. MAINS

New York

the sermon SUCKING BLACK HOLE
Why You Can't Remember on Monday What Your Minister Preached on Sunday

© 2015 DAVID R. MAINS.

Published in New York, New York, by Morgan James Publishing. Morgan James and The Entrepreneurial Publisher are trademarks of Morgan James, LLC.
www.MorganJamesPublishing.com

The Morgan James Speakers Group can bring authors to your live event. For more information or to book an event visit The Morgan James Speakers Group at
www.TheMorganJamesSpeakersGroup.com.

A **free** eBook edition is available
with the purchase of this print book.

CLEARLY PRINT YOUR NAME ABOVE IN UPPER CASE

Instructions to claim your free eBook edition:
1. Download the BitLit app for Android or iOS
2. Write your name in **UPPER CASE** on the line
3. Use the BitLit app to submit a photo
4. Download your eBook to any device

ISBN 978-1-63047-419-5 paperback
ISBN 978-1-63047-420-1 eBook
ISBN 978-1-63047-421-8 hardcover
Library of Congress Control Number:
2014949565

Cover Design by:
Rachel Lopez
www.r2cdesign.com

Interior Design by:
Bonnie Bushman
bonnie@caboodlegraphics.com

In an effort to support local communities, raise awareness and funds, Morgan James Publishing donates a percentage of all book sales for the life of each book to Habitat for Humanity Peninsula and Greater Williamsbu~~

Get involved today, visit
www.MorganJamesBuilds.com

Habitat
for Humanity®
Peninsula and
Greater Williamsburg
Building Partner

Dedicated to my oldest son
Randall John
who insisted repeatedly
that these concepts be put into a book
for those who listen to sermons
as well as those who preach them.

Table of Contents

Foreword

By Brian Mavis

Recently I pulled out my little red toolbox and started working on a plumbing project. I contorted my body beneath the sink and worked, and sweated, and banged away. But I was making no progress. No matter what I tried, I couldn't loosen a pipe that needed to be removed.

I called up my handyman neighbor, and he came over with his toolbox. He handed me a few tools, and in no time the pipe was removed and the rest of the plumbing project was done. I didn't have to work harder; in fact, I put less effort into it than before. The difference? I was given the right tools for the job.

In my role managing the largest-sermon preparation Web site in the world, I have read tens of thousands of sermons by preachers, crossing denominations, race, continents, gender and the age spectrum. I have a broad perspective on what the sermon landscape looks like, and I see the same thing over and over again: Pastors are struggling to put together life-changing sermons, and they are making very little progress because they are using a set of outdated and ill-fitted tools.

In a survey I conducted of hundreds of pastors, I asked the open-ended question, "What frustrates you the most about preaching?" By far the most frequent response was that there was a "lack of a connection and no life-change." And if you speak to people who listen to these sermons, they will tell you the same thing. Often they aren't sure what the sermon was even about, let alone what they are supposed to do to apply it.

Unfortunately, many preaching books aren't helping either. I've read hundreds of articles and books on preaching. Many of them are good and interesting, but not very helpful. My conclusions on most of them were, "This author doesn't really understand what is going on out there between the pulpit and the pew." But then I read a few articles that David Mains wrote about preaching and I thought, *This guy gets it! He has his pulse on what really is happening. He understands the real frustration of preachers and parishioners on Sunday mornings. And he has tools to fix it.*

Since then, David has become my friend and he has put his advice for preachers and parishioners in this book. With just four questions David gives pastors the tools to craft sermons that will make a difference in people's lives. With the same four questions, he gives listeners the tools to consider (not critique) what was preached so that they can apply the message in a life-changing way.

If you are a preacher who is struggling with sermon preparation, or you are a parishioner trying to get something from the sermons you hear, consider David Mains your handyman neighbor and this book his toolbox.

Acknowledgments

··

The Apostle Paul writes about once again being in *"the pains of childbirth"* for the church in Galatia (Galatians 4:19). So maybe I can use that feminine terminology and report that the "gestation period" for this book was the longest I have ever experienced—almost three years. Had it not been for the help of friends, a delivery may not have taken place.

Never have I felt more strongly about something I have written. Those who read my early efforts agreed that a "Black Hole" related to preaching in the church was truly a problem, but they were skittish about confronting it. Like David in 1 Samuel 26:9, they wondered, *"Who can lay a hand on the LORD's anointed and be guiltless?"*

Only when I was convinced that my motivation was to help ministries, not hurt them, was I comfortable proceeding. So I thank my early readers for making me be certain I was motivated by love for the church.

In time it was Silvia Lovette's fresh eyes that said where key changes needed to be made. Then the expert conceptual and line-editing skills of

George A. Koch came into play. Finally, when I no longer had it in me to again look at the manuscript, my good wife, Karen, added her final touches, for which I will be ever-grateful.

I believe the newborn is healthy and in time could even be a world-changer!

Chapter 1

The Sermon-Sucking Black Hole

···

B lack holes are strange invisible phenomena in outer space that form when stars collapse and their mass becomes highly compressed. This creates a localized gravitational force—an inward suction—powerful enough that even the star's light cannot escape. Larger black holes can exert an attraction so strong that nearby planets, comets and even other stars are pulled in over their rim—what astrophysicists term the "event horizon"—never to escape from this amazing vortex. As more and more objects are drawn in, the black hole grows in size and gravitational force.

By way of a limited example, our own Sun has a diameter of about 865,000 miles. To become a black hole it would have to collapse upon itself and be compressed to a diameter of less than four miles! Yet its dynamism would be such that it could just suck up nearby small heavenly bodies—*pflump!*

1

More typically, Sagittarius A*, the black hole in the Galactic Center of our Milky Way (yes, there is a black hole smack in the middle of our galaxy), measures 14 million miles across, and its gravitational pull is correspondingly much greater.

I'm not an astronomer, so I can't take you much further down this scientific path. Rather, I'm an ordained minister whose job it is to help others in my profession with their sermon- and service-planning.

It's my privilege to confer annually with hundreds of pastors, and, to my surprise, some of my colleagues infer that a "black hole" exists on their church property. They figure this sinister force is located somewhere between the pulpit and the parking lot, and it sucks up sermons! Ministers suggest this because parishioners who say as they leave the sanctuary, "Nice message, Reverend," moments later remember very little of what they heard. Something akin to a black hole swallows up the minister's sermon, so that before worshipers are halfway home, they have already forgotten most of what was said.

For me, this concern of the clergy is regularly underscored when I randomly ask friends later in the week what their minister preached about the previous Sunday. That may seem like an odd question, but these people know me and treat my inquiry as naturally as they would a car dealer asking, "How's the Mazda running?"

Invariably, they begin answering, quite confidently, "Oh, it was very good. Let's see, they preached about … isn't this funny, it escapes me right at the moment. *(long pause)* Hah, why isn't it coming back? *(longer pause)* For some reason, I can't seem to recall…!"

Even if I were to offer $100 just to remember the sermon subject, more often than not I would get to keep my money. *Why?*, I wonder, as do my pastor friends. *Have listeners thought even once about the sermon or homily since the benediction was given and the service was dismissed?*

Admittedly, people's memories are selective. They can remember who got voted off *American Idol* and why, but next to nothing regarding the Sunday service—what Scriptures were read, what songs were sung, what the choir's special music was. It's not that there aren't some remarkable Sunday messages being preached, because every so often someone will tell me about a special sermon or service element that impacted them, but generally the opposite is true. If you don't believe me, I challenge you to conduct some random sermon surveys of your own.

Recently a young man said, "Oh, Dr. Mains, I thought I might bump into you again and you would ask me what my priest talked about. So I paid extra attention at Mass to be ready just in case."

"Good," I replied. "What was last Sunday's topic?"

"Well, I'm actually talking about a week ago, but I didn't run into you."

"That's okay; what was your priest's talk about from a week ago then?"

Suddenly his mind went totally blank. He struggled to remember, but the topic seemed irretrievably lost. Because he had purposely put forth an effort to pay attention, I really wanted him to succeed.

"Take your time," I told him. "I'm not in a hurry."

Eventually he hung his head in defeat and confessed, "I just can't get it."

"I'm sorry," I responded.

Then he laughed, "One of these days I swear I'm going to be ready for you."

"Good," I assured him, genuinely meaning it. For now, however, the invisible Sermon-Sucking Black Hole had once again triumphed.

"Maybe your question is unfair," suggested a preaching colleague. "People live busy lives. If some Tuesday or Wednesday you asked me out of the blue what I preached about the previous weekend, I might have trouble coming up with the answer right there on the spot."

I decided to test his theory.

He was wrong. Pastors remember only too well. In fact, their recall is so exacting that I have had entire sermons repeated to me on the spot—to me, a congregation of one! Consequently, I've become rather reluctant to question that often the memory of ministers regarding their sermons.

A detective might conclude that the cause of the black hole is not in the pulpit, because the people who fill that sacred spot are not affected with sermon-memory loss. So let's start to look to the pews for the cause of this mnemonic deficiency.

Certainly there's much territory to explore here. On most Sundays this is where I sit, among the worshipers, rather than being "up on the platform." By the habits of a few people I've observed through the years, some would go home feeling empty even if Jesus Christ Himself were to honor the congregation with His presence. I'm referring to the individual who was up way too late the night before and now has trouble staying alert, or the modern-day Pharisee-type who knows everything there is to know about God and only comes to make sure the preacher remains doctrinally correct, or the family that habitually gets into a Sunday brouhaha on the way and is still bickering when they enter the sanctuary, even though they make a concerted effort to appear holy!

Seven decades in the church, however, prompt me to say that such individuals are the exception. Let me characterize the vast majority of Christians I have come to know. And I've worked with just about every group imaginable—Baptist, Methodist, Catholic, Lutheran, Reformed, AME, Salvation Army, Orthodox, Assemblies, Mennonite, Nazarene, Adventist, Anglican—the list is getting long, so I'll stop. I can report that for the most part these are decent, God-fearing folk who take their faith seriously and make it a point to be in church consistently, even when away on vacation. These are good people who long to hear God speak to their needs.

Yet they are also believers who have a hard time putting into words where they are spiritually, who struggle to maintain basic religious disciplines such as prayer or the regular study of Scripture, who have trouble putting into words specific ways they are maturing spiritually, and for that matter, who usually can't seem to remember what their spiritual leader said in the most recent sermon!

I'll reserve for later my suggestions for how to be a better worshiper. For now, I want to return to this matter of sermons becoming memorable. How do we counteract the force of this notorious black hole, which in my mind is the biggest problem faced by today's church? How can a sermon be relevant if its weekly impact on lives is minimal?

I want to make clear that this is a huge problem. It is not restricted to a given geographic region or only to certain denominations. It is across the board, affecting all branches of Christendom—Protestant, Catholic and Orthodox. This flaw is endemic to the churches of North America. There are exceptions, but not nearly as many as one would like to think.

This point must be understood, because I have conversed with too many ministers who agree with my premise, but assume it's the pastor down the street being referred to and not them. As a reader of this book, you need to realize that from my perspective, I am probably writing about your church! If you don't think so, you'd better make sure, because all too many congregations across North America are struggling and don't have nearly the clout they once did.

I've spoken with countless pastors who are deeply concerned that attendance is down, as is giving; that they don't have the volunteer workers they once did; and that when a kid's soccer game is scheduled for Sunday morning, church attendance for that family takes a backseat. There's a lot of hashing over of contemporary problems related to the church. But very few people seem to conclude or realize that what's preached from the pulpit often might not be all that relevant, helpful or motivating—and that until this number-one problem is resolved, nothing truly significant is going to change.

Past surveys reveal that the messages most remembered by those in the pews—don't be shocked—are the ones given when all the kids are asked to come to the front, *i.e.* the children's sermon. I suspect this is because these presentations are short, deal with one main idea, use simple words and visuals, engage the children in some kind of response, and help the little listeners apply the important lesson to their lives—"See what happens when we tell lies. Do you think you will tell any lies this week?"

In contrast, common complaints from parishioners about "big-people" sermons include the following:

- too many ideas
- too much spiritual jargon / too theological
- too few illustrations
- too much about the problem, not enough about the solution
- too unrelated to people's lives
- too long and/or boring

The truth is, pastors know these criticisms better than their people do. Most ministers I meet have read the books, listened to the experts, tried all kinds of new methods, diligently searched their own souls, and despaired over the statistics that reveal sermons are not as effective as they once were in changing people's lives. I'm convinced most clergy are doing the best they know how, and are the very ones most concerned that their listeners can't remember what's preached.

My contention is that preachers need the help of their people. This is so important, it merits repeating: *Preachers need the help of those in their congregation.* Unfortunately, parishioners don't know yet how to provide what's needed, and preachers don't know what to ask for. That's the mission of this short book—to teach both sides some simple but effective and proven helps.

For those readers who have never heard of me, let me give a short autobiography to explain why this preaching gap between the pulpit and the pew is so important to me. In 50-some years of ministry, I have known the joys and sorrows of a long inner-city and multiracial pastorate; before that, I was an associate at the historic Moody Memorial Church in Chicago. I subsequently invested 20 years in preaching on religious radio with *The Chapel of the Air* six days a week over some 500 outlets, and our national daily TV show *You Need to Know* won the National Religious Broadcasters' "Television Program Producer of the Year" award in 1995. I have created materials called *50-Day Spiritual Adventures*, used by tens of thousands of churches and millions of individual Christians; been a guest professor at seminaries here and overseas; counseled with committed pastors; written or co-authored many books; edited the *Study Bible for Personal Revival* (Zondervan); worked on joint projects with parachurch ministries (e.g., Promise Keepers, Mission America, Youth For Christ); was commissioned to write sermons for the Canadian film *The Gospel of John,* and had some 36,000 ministers request a copy of the sermon series I wrote on Mel Gibson's film *The Passion of the Christ.*

Over the decades, in all these fields of ministry, my suspicion has been overwhelmingly verified, that most people are not remembering or applying in practical ways the messages they hear on Sundays. So let's begin to work together to help solve this mystery of what's happening to our sermons.

Some astronomers estimate that black holes make up as much as one-third of all the matter in our galaxy, the Milky Way. That's amazing! We can't see black holes, because by their very nature they "swallow" light, but their presence has been verified by complicated mathematical formulae. The effect of black holes upon regions in the universe has been observed with powerful modern telescopes in observatories worldwide.

Our problem won't be quite that hard to solve, but it won't be a cakewalk, either. Pastors are often reluctant to invite parishioners to help them in their sermon- and service-preparation. And most people in the pew don't realize how integral they are to finding a solution to the Sermon-Sucking Black Hole. But I have seen how the pulpit/pew combination can be an incredibly powerful team, and I have every confidence in it.

Fortunately, we're working with a system that's collapsing like an old star under its own weight. The traditional three-point-lecture format that held audiences spellbound in generations past is no longer pertinent in the same way to modern people. We need to come up with new approaches that will once again release the light of the Gospel message. Together, I believe we can do it.

One Last Thought

"I guess I don't relate to your book," a friend from another state told me the first time we talked about my "manuscript." He continued, "The minister we have now is one of the best preachers I've ever sat under. He talks about current issues. He's funny, but he can also be quite serious. And he sticks right to the Bible."

"Consider yourself fortunate," I told him, and moved our conversation on to another topic.

The next time we saw each other, he was the one to bring up the Black Hole. "I got to thinking about our earlier talk," he said, "and as much as I like to listen to our pastor preach, I retain almost nothing of what he says. I don't know why, but once the Sunday service is over, there's very little, if anything, that actually sticks with me."

He had been happy before I talked about my concerns. Maybe I should have just kept my thoughts to myself. But that's not who I am.

All this is to request that you not be too quick to make up your mind about what you're reading. This is not about whether you are loyal to your pastor or priest. Hopefully that's not even a question.

Rather, this book is about average parishioners doing everything possible to maximize the effectiveness of what they hear preached. If that's already happening, I'm thrilled for you. If it's not, I want to be of help.

Chapter 2

The Best Sermon Judges

....

A foundation once requested that I be one of several judges in a national sermon contest, with some rather significant monies to be awarded the winners. I confess I was conflicted in deciding whether to participate. You see, one of my deepest convictions is that the best judge of whether a sermon is effective is *not* an ordained minister like myself, whose whole life has been involved with "the things of the Lord."

Nor would I recommend some of my friends who are highly qualified, long-time seminary professors at institutions where up-and-coming future preachers are trained. That does not mean I do not hold the highest regard for these teachers, because I am often intellectually and emotionally moved when opportunities come my way to hear them open God's Word.

In addition, though I'm not a huge fan of the religious media, there are certain personalities whose messages never cease to capture my interest. I recall decades back, as a college student, watching Catholic Bishop Fulton Sheen on television and, even as a Protestant, wanting to applaud every time he concluded a presentation. I loved to hear Oswald Hoffman on the *Lutheran Hour* radio show, and C.M. Ward with the Assemblies of God, talking about his listeners meeting Jesus at the long, long altar that, by means of radio, literally stretched across the country. I could envision this as he painted it with his wonderful words. Billy Graham has always been one of my spiritual heroes. I admired him when he was a fiery young preacher and then even more as a seasoned and respected religious statesman (now suffering from Parkinson's), preaching from his open Bible from ever-so-many strategic spots around the globe.

Chuck Swindoll has more than once kept me sitting in my car even after I arrived at my destination, because I wanted to hear the conclusion to what he was preaching. T.D. Jakes is one of several African-American ministers whose amazing style I find matched by his equally amazing intellect. And there are others on my list.

Because I travel a lot, I have been mesmerized by certain unique speakers at major conventions such as the Christian Booksellers or the National Religious Broadcasters. In my memory, I can still hear the high-pitched voice and impassioned pleas of apologist Francis Schaeffer. In my estimation, Tom Skinner had the makings of a modern-day prophet raised up from the street gangs by the Lord Himself. When Dr. Sandra Wilson spoke about psychological issues, her insights went right to my heart and exorcised several of my all-too-many dysfunctional traits.

Leonard Ravenhill was a friend whose hot heart for revival stoked that same fire in me. I see many of the classic evidences of awakening in certain mega-church ministries, and can't deny the strong impulse to share the Gospel that marks the messages of pastors like Bill Hybels at the huge Willow Creek Community Church in Illinois.

Nevertheless, if I want to know beyond a shadow of a doubt whether a given sermon is a real winner, these are not the kind of "experts" I'd go to. My deep-seated belief is that the people in the pews (or, nowadays, the chairs, theatre seats, whatever) should be the ones who ultimately determine sermons' immediate and long-range positive effects. Let me repeat: The layperson knows best whether a sermon is effective in bringing about personal life change.

Granted, listeners need simple guidelines to be able to do this. Otherwise, they might be unduly swayed by the preacher's passion or humor. They need a methodology that helps them decide whether they feel truly inspired, learn anything interesting, or just plain momentarily enjoy the experience.

The truth is that none of these elements listed above (which are common themes laypeople use to evaluate sermons) is really paramount. The real purpose sermons are preached is to help people encounter and then become more like Jesus, to come under His authority or kingship. That is, sermons should help listeners enter Christ's Kingdom and then mature in that new relationship as His highly privileged subjects. Preaching is not primarily to display a communication talent, to capture people through a sparkling personality, or to gather support for a given cause or project. John the Baptist had it right centuries ago when he said of Christ, *"He must increase, and I must decrease."*

As a young minister I was impressed reading about the powerful black preacher John Jasper, who ministered after the Civil War at the large Sixth Mount Zion Baptist Church in Richmond. "Does that mean there are five other Mount Zion Baptist Churches?" he was asked. "No suh," he replied, "we jes' liked de name!"

As told in the book *Rhapsody In Black: The Life Story of John Jasper* by Richard Ellsworth Day, Jasper was not an educated pastor in terms of formal training. But he had a captivating way with words and a deep love for his Lord. Sermon titles were topics like "Whar Sin

Come From?", "Dem Sebun Wimmin" and "De Stone Cut Out ub de Mount'n." White folk often came to his church for the spirited music, the empowered preaching and for "an evening's entertainment." A buzz of chatter characterized these curiosity-seekers when they first arrived, but after the service as they left the sanctuary in an uncharacteristic hush, the comment heard most often was, "John Jasper loves Jesus." Then another would say softly in response, "Yes, John Jasper certainly does love Jesus." Like the New Testament phenomenon of Jesus' day, John the Baptist, this John also came to bear witness to the light. That's how it always is with truly effective sermons!

Speaking from the preacher's viewpoint, I'd say the most daunting assignment is to attempt to reflect what Jesus Himself would preach were He to take His place in the pulpit as rightful head of the church. My habit, when I'm completing preparation on a sermon, is to go over it one last time for Jesus, to picture whether or not what I'm saying has His approval. Sometimes I'm convicted that my message is not as strong as it should be, that I've backed away from making clear what the One I represent really wants spoken. Other times in that final "go-over," I realize my words are not as compassionate as He would want them. More than once I have found too much of self and not enough of Christ, and I try to make the necessary last-minute adjustments. As I age, I'm pleased that more often than in earlier years I have this feeling I'm closer to the target, and I experience a wonderful sense of His approval. I'll never be what Christ is, but to believe I have His blessing is a great thrill.

Part of what should happen under exceptional preaching is that the Savior's voice starts to be heard alongside the words of His human servant. That's when sermons are at their best. It's what I listen for, and when it happens, it's what I appreciate most.

Don't misunderstand. I'm not describing some kind of aesthetic experience. When Jesus talks it doesn't necessarily make people comfortable. Just the opposite is often true. More often than not Christ's words anger listeners, issue a challenge beyond what people are ready to hear, or even put them under deep conviction. Of course, His words can also bring great hope, release people from great burdens, or let them discover that elusive, priceless pearl they have long been seeking and now realize is theirs for the taking.

Back to my quandary that began this chapter—regarding a foundation's invitation to judge the preaching finals—if I said yes to being a judge, would I be able to discern this voice of Christ when reading submitted sermon manuscripts? And were there untrained people in the pew who were equally capable of doing this?

As I mentioned earlier, beyond just encountering Jesus, listeners should ultimately be motivated to become more like Him. So sermons are prepared and preached to change people's lives.

Biblical information is important. So is spiritual inspiration. Sermon illustrations keep people's attention. Humor is wonderful, especially if it's at the speaker's expense. Timing is critical, as is the way a sermon is structured. The bottom line, however, is the effect these combined elements have on people's lives. Are those in attendance becoming more and more like the Son of God? Will people look at the laity and say, "Norm and Norma Christian love Jesus. They certainly do love Jesus"?

Perhaps the greatest dilemma we face in the church is the body of statistics that reveal there is little distinction in the lifestyles of born-again believers and non-churched individuals. These survey results are quoted so frequently as a warning, they have almost become cliché. So let's not belabor the point, but just look at one alarming reality that hints at an iceberg lurking beneath the surface of our everyday lives. The Barna Research Group found that one in four American adults has had at least one divorce. That's not particularly new, but what is new is the surprising outcome to emerge from the study that reveals born-again Christians are *more* likely than non-Christians to have a marital split. The numbers state that though just 11% of the adult population is currently divorced, 25% of all adults have experienced at least one divorce in their lifetime. Among born-again Christians, 27% are currently or previously divorced, compared to 24% among non-born-again adults. What is happening in our faith communities when so basic a structure as the Christian family is being riddled with the alienation and ruin inherent in marital collapse? Why is the preaching in the pulpit not being integrated in such a way that the spoken Word helps Christian couples (and the church communities that should be supporting them) prevent these failures?

A sermon has to go beyond correct doctrine, as important as it is. God's Truth has to have a tangible effect on lives. Shouldn't there be a clear difference between being a nice American, enjoying all the privileges that our citizenship affords, and living as a committed believer, who even before getting to heaven submits here on Earth to Christ's righteous reign? Here again is where I believe ministers have their greatest frustration. Whatever the reason, sermons don't seem to have that much impact on behavior. One nationally known pastor honestly bemoaned this problem to a group of colleagues: "I have been preaching in my church for over 20 years, and my people are no more different now than when I started." What an honest and terrible appraisal. The Sermon-Sucking Black Hole is a terrifying phenomenon faced by even the best of the best!

Obviously, the party listening to what's preached is in the best position to judge whether the message he/she hears is accomplishing what's intended, and if not, why not. Believe me, people in the pew can analyze that better than those in the pulpit. So why not invite lay folk to act as sermon judges? But how will that happen when their listening habits prepare them *not* to remember what's been preached?

It was at this point I knew how to respond to the request from the foundation that asked me to judge at their sermon contest.

When it comes to talking about the effectiveness of sermons, it's common for church folk to comment about their pastor's preaching being dynamic or dull, deep or shallow, heady or a tad emotional, plus all the stops in between. But the last thing in the world most people will include in their evaluation is a personal reflection on how *their* lives are being affected. Are they still growing spiritually because of their pastor's sermons? If so, specifically how? If not, why not?

I concluded that the average layperson was not yet ready for a sermon-judging assignment. So I accepted the invitation. I have honed some skills in this discipline. At the same time, I made a personal commitment to draw upon my years of experience and write down in a book a few simple guidelines, regarding this sermon-memory concern, that will begin to train all adults who go to church. And it's a one-size-fits-all model.

Scientists talk about constructing formulae that are elegant in their simplicity. At first glance, Einstein's equation $E = mc^2$ seems simple enough. But his book Relativity: The Special and the General Theory—which was written for laypeople who, as he explains in the preface, "are interested in the theory, but who are not conversant with the mathematical apparatus of theoretic physics"—gives even the intelligent reader pause. Despite the back-cover copy—"Apparent throughout is Einstein's remarkable ability to penetrate directly to the heart of the subject in a way virtually everyone can understand"—one look at the titles, and a quick review of the short pages makes a reader aware of the confusing world of quantum mechanics, physics, astrophysics and mathematics that must first be mastered before this formula can be truly comprehensible.

Imagine the leap Einstein's contemporaries were forced to make who did not have decades to absorb the stunning implications of the special and the general theories of relativity. By the way, without them, little of modern-day astronomy or physics could have proceeded, including the discovery of the existence of black holes (and, consequently, the nature of stars). In 1919, the distinguished astrophysicist Sir Arthur Eddington mounted an expedition to observe a total eclipse of the Sun, to test a prediction of general relativity—namely, that light would bend near a massive star near the Sun. When he reported his observations "gave a result agreeing with Einstein," Eddington's fame became world-renown.

A year later he bumped into a notable physicist at the Royal Society. The man exclaimed, "Well! Professor Eddington, you must be one of the three people in the world who understands Relativity." When Eddington demurred, the other man insisted, "Don't be modest." Eddington's famous reply (with which he often regaled dinner parties) was, "On the contrary! I am wondering who the third person is!"

I would like to offer a proposal for conquering the Sermon-Sucking Black Hole that at first glance appears rather simple; it is a general theory of communication that can improve the lasting and life-changing impact of what pastors preach (without changing their preferred style of preaching). In addition, it will radically alter the way listeners hear. And this tool, this one-size-fits-all tool, can be used as a simple-but-effective survey that will quickly show communicators what people have heard, retained and are ready to apply (or if, indeed, they have forgotten the contents of the sincere labor of pastors Sunday after Sunday).

My goal, unlike Sir Arthur Eddington, is not to gloat in some esoteric brilliance, but to share a sermon-development and listener-aptitude tool that can even be understood by the millions of people who still go to church each Sunday. The first part is a "General Theory of Sermon Evaluation" that contains four simple questions and can revolutionize the way preachers preach and listeners listen. The second part is a "Special Theory of Pastor and Laypeople Dialogue" that will radicalize how sermons are constructed and delivered, then evaluated, remembered and applied.

The number of people in this nation who attend the Lord's House each week is still quite high. It dwarfs the aggregate figures for sporting events, theatergoers, rock concerts, you name it. But this huge population segment still lacks an agreed-upon way to quickly get a handle on what's being said by clergy. Let's look at a constructive and meaningful way to do this.

One Last Thought

Right about now you're probably thinking, "If I'm potentially such a great judge of sermons, why is it no one has ever asked for my opinion? And if someone ever did, how come I haven't the slightest idea what I would say?"

"Hopefully the day will soon come," I respond, "when church leaders will not only solicit your thoughts, but value them as well. Regarding what you would say…"

"Come on," you interrupt, "doesn't a person need training of some kind to do this? I mean, I wouldn't know how to judge a dog show, much less be able to evaluate how a trained minister handles God's Word."

"Well, yes," I pick up where I left off, "you will need to know what to listen for. That's where we're headed in our journey together. Without a track to run on, your judging could take off in a thousand different directions."

"But what do I know about public speaking?" you protest. "I'm just not comfortable with the assumptions you're making."

"And you're starting to make assumptions *I'm* not comfortable with," I laughingly reply. "I don't want you to evaluate talent like someone might for *American Idol*. What you're judging is the affect of a minister's words on your life. How impacting will they be? That I believe you can do. But don't anticipate problems until we at least get to the next chapter. Okay?"

"All right," you agree, still not convinced.

Chapter 3

Two of the Four Simple Sermon-Evaluation Questions

∙∙

H undreds and hundreds of times I have had the privilege of speaking to ministers on the topic of preaching. Often members of their congregation will attend these sessions with them. I much prefer having multiple teaching sessions with the same group. Unfortunately, most of the time I only have one chance to say what is on my mind.

For a one-time lecture my bottom line is this: Immediately after a sermon has been preached, those who heard it should be able to answer four simple questions. The first, and by far the easiest, is: What was the subject of the sermon?

As basic as this sounds, often hearers are unable to come up with the answer. Allow me to make a distinction: Telling me the text your pastor preached on is not the same as identifying the subject of the sermon.

For example, a person could respond, "Our minister's message was from Psalm 1."

My comment would be, "I grant you that Psalm 1 is short and only has six verses. But they still cover quite a bit of ground. So what direction did your pastor take? Again, what was the subject of the sermon?"

A well-trained minister will look for an obvious subject. Let's try it, to get a feel for what I'm describing. Read Psalm 1, then decide what you think the basic subject is:

> *¹ Blessed is the man who does not walk in the counsel of the wicked or stand in the way of sinners or sit in the seat of mockers.*
> *² But his delight is in the law of the* Lord, *and on his law he meditates day and night.*
> *³ He is like a tree planted by streams of water, which yields its fruit in season and whose leaf does not wither. Whatever he does prospers.*
> *⁴ Not so the wicked! They are like chaff that the wind blows away.*
> *⁵ Therefore the wicked will not stand in the judgment, nor sinners in the assembly of the righteous.*
> *⁶ For the* Lord *watches over the way of the righteous, but the way of the wicked will perish.*

Don't read any more until you have decided what the subject of this Psalm is.

I used this passage recently in a pastor's workshop. Within a few minutes the majority felt the subject was something like "The Person Blessed by God" (verse 1). A few opted for "The Way of the Righteous" (verse 6). Either subject would be a legitimate preaching approach, and the psalm is written in such a fashion that the two ideas are almost interchangeable.

Then I asked the group whether their congregations would rather hear a message about "How to Be Blessed by God" or "How to Live Righteously Before God." How would you have responded?

The entire class felt their people would vote for the former, "How to Be Blessed by God," so that's the topic we chose to work with. I'll use this passage as my basic text as we look later at the remaining three questions.

The other day a friend told me, "Our minister preached about Peter getting out of the boat and walking to Christ on the water."

"That's a great text," I responded. "It's found in Matthew 14 and also in Mark and John. But why did he choose that passage? He must have had something in mind other than just retelling a familiar story. So what do you think his sermon subject was?" This individual was not able to say.

Am I making sense to you, my reader?

You see, that given preaching subject could be something like, "Lessons Learned in the Midst of a Storm" or "Exercising Faith Even When You're Afraid." Framing the subject attractively is what gives the listener a reason to keep on paying attention. If the subject is not compelling, the rest of the sermon is not likely to be either.

It's not infrequent when talking to someone after a service to hear, "I'm not sure what the subject of the sermon was, but I can give you the three points of the outline," and they proceed to do just that.

"So what subject do you think these three points fit under?" I press them. Hopefully they will get it right, because I sincerely want them to. Usually they can't.

"I remember one of the illustrations" is another common remark. That's good—at least this listener remembered *something*. But again, if a person can't get the answer to a question as basic as, "What was the subject of the sermon?", there's little wonder the Sermon-Sucking Black Hole has such an incredible winning record.

For literally decades, I have asked church people my 4 simple sermon-evaluation questions. I estimate that, if given a surprise test at the end of a service, in the average congregation, only about one-third would get the sermon subject right, roughly one-third would come up with a wrong answer, and the other third wouldn't have the faintest idea because they really weren't listening all that closely, or maybe the subject was never made clear. Possibly the minister divided the sermon time between the six verses of Psalm 1 (if that was the text), and no one point seemed to have that much of an emphasis.

If you think I'm way off-base regarding your church, an easy way to find out is to conduct your own random quiz as the people are being dismissed. Ask a few of your friends, or take a moment to gently drill some Sunday dinner guests. Should you want an even-better look at this matter of inadequate sermon-recall, do a quick phone survey on the next Tuesday or Wednesday!

It doesn't matter to me whether your pastor preaches topically or verse-by-verse, is a marvelous storyteller, or dresses up like Moses and delivers the sermon in character. If hearers can't answer as elementary a question as "What was the sermon subject?", then to quote Paul Newman from *Cool Hand Luke*, "What we've got here is a (major) failure to communicate."

So what was the subject of one of your minister's recent sermons? Not the Bible passage, or a great illustration, but the sermon subject? If you can't recall, pay special attention the next time you are in church, and see if you can come up with an answer.

Let's go on to Question 2 in this sermon-evaluation tool. Simple sermon-evaluation question number two is: What response was called for?

A sermon needs to go beyond mere information. At its best it's a challenge to be more Christ-like. Unfortunately, more often than not, those listening aren't really sure what's expected of them. I suspect a vast majority of the sermons preached in our churches don't actually ask for a clear response. My conclusions come from my years of major interest in the Sermon-Sucking Black Hole. I've critiqued and edited hundreds of sermons from pastors for decades for our annual *50-Day Spiritual Adventure* and *Advent Celebration* products; I've worked with pastors in the Mainstay Ministers Conferences (as many as 137 conferences a year); I've listened to hundreds of sermons in churches and classrooms. The vast majority do not have a clear response. Even the finalists in the sermon contest I judged (the 100 best sermons submitted) largely failed to ask for a clear response from their listeners. And as you know by now, I've waylaid all kinds of unsuspecting laypeople with my four simple sermon-evaluation questions. If few can give me the subject of their pastor's recent sermon, even fewer can say the response called for.

Usually the response is going to be right there in the chosen text. By way of example, let's return to Psalm 1 about "The Person Who Is Blessed by God." Here are verses 1 and 2 again:

> *¹ Blessed is the man who does not walk in the counsel of the wicked or stand in the way of sinners or sit in the seat of mockers.*
> *² But his delight is in the law of the LORD, and on his law he meditates day and night.*

Restated, the person who wants God's blessing will get counsel from the right source and avoid input from all the wrong sources. Make sense? (1) We want to get counsel from God's law, and (2) we want to avoid advice from mockers, the wicked and sinners. That's the desired response tucked into this passage.

Is this response relevant? Do people today regularly make decisions based on input from questionable sources? If I was working with a roomful of pastors, I would ask them to give me some specific examples of negative influences.

"Doing business based totally on what Donald Trump advises" may be one idea.

"Teens listen to the lyrics of much of today's popular music and absorb its values."

"Buying into popular business magazines' focus on the fact that earning and investing money is life's highest goal."

These are good answers, and there are more negative examples that could quickly be given. "What about getting input from good sources?" I would pursue next. "Generally speaking, are church people good at delighting in the law of the Lord? What do you pastors think?"

"The Psalm talks about meditating on the law of the Lord or on Scripture. Most of my folk struggle to find time for that."

"Too many of my people base the appearance and use of their homes on what's in popular magazines instead of on biblical principles of hospitality or Jesus' teachings in passages like Luke 14:12–14, *'When you give a luncheon or dinner, do not invite your friends, your brothers or relatives, or your rich neighbors; if you do, they may invite you back and so you will be repaid. But when you give a banquet, invite the poor, the crippled, the lame, the blind, and you will be blessed. Although they cannot repay you, you will be repaid at the resurrection of the righteous.'*"

"Group Bible studies have been hard for me to get started. But a couple of them seem to finally be making it."

The passage is clear, however, and if Psalm 1 is the text being preached, the response called for is one that's hard to miss. Those who want God's blessing should get their counsel from the right source and be careful about questionable ones.

Because a given response might not be all that well-received, is that a warning to back away from making clear what the passage calls for? Not if a minister goes over the sermon one final time with Jesus before preaching it to the congregation. Chances are the pastor will be instructed by the Holy Spirit to preach it anyway, and with all the weight of heaven behind it.

What about those listening? It's their job to discern whether the challenge is truly biblical. If so, they've heard "a word from the Lord." What they do with it is up to them. But the calling of the man or woman of God has been fulfilled. What happens is a replay of Ezekiel 2:7, *"You must speak my words to them, whether they listen or fail to listen."*

However, when preachers don't make clear what Jesus wants said, it's a sad day for everyone. If they open up a topic and make it interesting but don't emphasize the response called for or implied in the passage, the problem is doubly compounded.

One of the obvious qualifications of being a leader is having followers. If nobody does what the pastor tells them, the minister isn't much of a leader. He or she may have several degrees and a title, but if they say "jump" and nobody does, there's a serious breakdown somewhere. The same is true if the pastor finishes preaching and the hearers are honestly confused as to what's expected of them.

This is an admitted generalization, but my guess is that 80% of the time I hear clergy preach, I cannot figure out the desired response. I listen closely, but it just isn't there. The points are clear. Usually they're interesting and timely. The delivery is polished and has obviously been practiced. The sermon just doesn't go anywhere. The hearer does not know why that text is being preached and what is expected from him/her.

Is this why people often don't know what to say when they leave the sanctuary? Meeting the pastor at the door, they mumble something like, "Thank you. I believe I feel more like I do now then when I came."

"What's that supposed to mean?" the pastor wonders.

"And what's all that supposed to have meant?" muses the attendee, opening the car door and beginning the drive home.

One Last Thought

If you always knew ahead of time what the questions were going to be, to a large degree the fear of taking tests would be eliminated. With a little concentrated study you could easily pass the American History midterm or your driver's exam.

The reason I believe you can do a great job of evaluating sermons is that I'm telling you up front what the key questions are. You just need to listen for the answers.

On top of that, if you can't rather easily figure out what the subject of a given sermon is, it's not like you failed. More likely it's the sermon that has come up short. How stress-relieving is that!

If you somehow miss the response desired, even though you were attentively listening for it, you don't get the low grade; the sermon does! What a great arrangement, right?

True, it could partially be your fault for not paying closer attention. For thinking about business matters, family problems, sports, shopping, or just letting your mind wander aimlessly. But I'm believing better of you than to allow that to happen once you're in church.

And yes, there are two more questions you haven't been told yet. But those aren't really any harder to grasp than the first two were.

So, restated, knowing the basics related to what you should expect to get from a good sermon greatly simplifies your task. Whether you add a plus or a minus to your final grade is pretty much up to you.

Chapter 4

Do You Know How to Do That?

· ·

A family friend made a midweek stop at my office. From earlier conversations I knew he was looking for a church home. So I asked if he had found a place yet where he thought he might fit. "Oh, yes," he informed me. "For several months now I've been going to the _____ church, and there's a lot I really like about it."

"What did your minister preach on last Sunday?" I asked, resorting almost automatically to simple question number one.

"Let's see," he said, pausing only slightly. Then, to my amazement, within just a couple of seconds he had the answer. "He just started a new series on the book of Acts. This Sunday was week two and chapter two. So he talked about the great sermon Peter preached on the day of Pentecost."

I couldn't believe it. Almost instantly my friend had come up with the answer. What he gave me, of course, was his pastor's text and what that passage was about. But then, I hadn't asked my question correctly. I

27

should have inquired, "What was the subject of the sermon?" But rather than back up and start over, I decided to move on to simple question number two. I was anxious to see whether he could answer that one as quickly. "Do you recall the response your minister was looking for?" I tossed out.

Bang! Just like that, he nailed it! "He wants us to be a bold witness for Jesus."

Incredible! Hardly anyone ever responds with fast, precise answers like that, especially three days after the service!

So ... on to simple question number three. Question #3 is: "Do you know how to do that—how to be a bold witness for Jesus?"

That's when I pushed him into a dead end. After a while, with a rather embarrassed grin, he reluctantly admitted, "I haven't a clue!"

This epitomizes another major problem with all too many sermons— they tell people what to do, but fail to explain to people *how* to go about doing it. The messages aren't useful if they lack concrete guidance. I can't emphasize enough that the sermon really begins to be heard when preachers give practical ideas for implementing their themes. It is at this point listeners begin to think strategically. *Maybe I can get back into Bible study if I use my kids' comic-book Bible!*

In the article "Stick It in Your Ear! Preaching as an Oral-Aural Transaction," Neil Alexander writes, "People are not changed when words are spoken, but when they are heard. ... [This] is a profound idea for the preacher to embrace." I would stretch the concept a little further and add this: People are not changed simply when words are spoken, but when the words are heard *and then used to transform the way they are living.* That **transformation** comes through applying understandable, doable how-tos. This is an even more profound idea for the preacher to embrace.

Over their years in the pastorate, ministers have usually learned to live out the various spiritual responses called for in Scripture, but they assume their people know how to as well. When they preach something like "be a bold witness for Jesus," they figure the how-to is understood by all. The truth is, most believers haven't even begun to master such specialized skills.

During a closed brainstorming session with some church folk, I once asked, "If you could tell your pastor one thing, what would it be?" One gentleman responded that his minister needed to understand there is a big difference between WHAT and HOW. I asked him to be more specific.

"It's like when my wife tells me to fix the upstairs toilet. 'It's leaking at the base,' she informs me. So that's the WHAT she wants me to do. I clearly understand the WHAT. It's the HOW I'm hung up on. 'At the longest, my dad could fix any toilet in an hour,' she badgers me. 'So what do you mean you don't know how?' Two dreadful hours later, with water dripping through the floor to the downstairs and a cracked toilet bowl at my feet, she realizes I'm not exactly a union plumber. I'm not self-taught in this skill like her dad was. I'm basically inept! Now toilets are a topic we avoid talking about if possible."

His comments made sense. WHAT is one thing; HOW is something else entirely. Too many sermons just stop once the response has been clearly stated. "Now get out there and fix those toilets," the minister essentially says. It's like this gentleman's wife: No practical how-to is being provided to help. One of the reasons is that the how-to is seldom found in the biblical text. And most of the ministers I know feel most comfortable when they can quote specific Scriptures to back up their words.

The reason how-tos aren't generally found in the Bible is because times and cultures change. How to "fix a toilet" in Old Testament days differs considerably from the way one would go about it now (though Leviticus recommends a shovel and some distance from the camp!). Put in a more serious context, how to meditate on God's Word will be different for an illiterate first-century Bedouin compared to a 21st-century, sophisticated high-riser who seldom has enough quiet for meditating even at home because of constant background noise from the neighbors' television across the hall.

The man's plumbing illustration takes us back to Psalm 1, which calls for people who want God's blessing to get their counsel from the right sources—remember? These folk should learn to meditate on God's Word. Can the average church member really pull this off without additional input? Hey, we don't have a predominate number of seminary graduates sitting out there in the pews, taking everything in. Many in the average congregation don't even have a rudimentary knowledge of the books of the Bible. If they spend a couple minutes a day in prayer, they're doing great. The very thought of meditating sounds overwhelming, even a bit new-age. So it would be quite helpful for the preacher to use some of the sermon time to spell out baby steps for fledgling meditators.

Maybe the church bulletin could include a sheet with a related Scripture passage with questions to think about for each of the next six days. The church could buy some basic books on Christian meditation, and lend them to people who want to learn more. A man or woman in the congregation who's grown in this practice over the past several years could share a testimony. A special class for beginners might be established. Specific tools, teaching events and training certainly need to be provided to help bridge the gap for the novices seeking to improve.

According to Psalm 1, people who want to be blessed by God not only need to get their counsel from the right source, they should be careful about being unduly influenced by questionable sources. Think about it. Do church attendees show all that much discernment when it comes to things like the movies they go to, the DVDs they rent, the music they listen to, the magazines and books they read, the TV shows they watch, the friends they confide in?

Some do and some don't—right? Then what how-to could a preacher give that will help more people to use greater discernment?

Certainly various congregants could share their critiquing techniques for deciding what to watch and what to ignore. Some families are quite good at evaluating what they see. These parents and their kids have learned to quickly determine when Christian values are endorsed or violated. There must be discriminating viewers somewhere in most churches who have figured out what is appropriate (or not) about shows like *The Apprentice* or the *Real Housewives* franchise. Unfortunately, all too often their successful secrets remain private and are not helpful for the broader Body of Christ.

Let me repeat: It's fairly easy for a preacher to quickly get into the sermon *subject* and the *response* being called for. It's the *how-to* that takes extra help and sermon time to develop. Sadly, most sermons never even mention how to do what's needed to effect life transformation. The hearers' minds have not been engaged with intriguing practicalities. The tragic habit of listening has become one of hearing and forgetting.

So hear me now. Unless change comes in regard to these matters, the American church has little hope of surviving! Give it a couple more generations of the same old, same old, and I prophesy that our sanctuaries will be as empty as Europe's!

A couple decades back, the battle lines in the Church were drawn over the issue of music. It was a bloody war that still continues in some settings. But new instruments started to appear, like guitars and (would you believe) drums! Song leaders slowly faded into oblivion, and worship teams replaced them. Instead of a hymn here and there in the service, large blocks of time were opened up for sustained worship, often featuring new songs that were sung over and over until learned. People stood more than before and began lifting their hands in praise. Hymnals were put aside for words projected on front walls or screens.

The revolution left many wounded, but in the end, the younger element had its way.

What I see on the horizon is "The Mother of All Church Wars." This time it will center on preaching, and it will make the earlier music conflicts seem like child's play. The *once-liberal* generation that changed the church musically, now having grown older, could become the *now-conservative* ones who fight hard to maintain the status quo and hold the line in terms of what they think biblical preaching should be. Having moved into church leadership positions, if they prove too intransigent they may end up winning in the church, but that will allow the enemy to be triumphant in the truly important theatre of battle, and the Sermon-Sucking Black Hole will have won the day.

Hundreds of thousands of sermons are preached each weekend, and most really aren't accomplishing much. People still come and listen, but spiritually, they leave about the same as when they arrived. After they get home, many of them can't even answer simple questions like, "What was the subject of the sermon?" "What response was called for?" "What practical help was offered regarding how to do this?" So the message is quickly forgotten, and the sinister Black Hole is truly black because it's an enemy-dominated stronghold that to date has hardly been challenged.

Before leaving this matter of how-tos and introducing one final simple question, let me make an observation. Without more input from their people, I don't think most pastors will be able to come up with workable how-tos. The gulf between the life of the average minister and that of his/her people is much bigger than most realize.

It would be to everyone's benefit if, once a week, pastors scheduled time to drop in—on a classroom or office, or studio or repair shop, or factory or retail outlet—places where the average congregant works— just to observe what goes on. You can tell from their sermons that many preachers have lost touch with such places.

This disconnect is probably not uniquely a church problem. Most likely a physician doesn't identify all that much with patient concerns until personally being hospitalized for something serious and billed for the services!

I recall as a young man working under a nationally known pastor. For a change of pace, he'd curtailed his world travels to take a large church. My wife and I arranged a number of small socials with a dozen or so members each time so he could get to know them. The first evening, however, consisted of the new pastor being introduced, then taking the rest of the night to regale his unknown parishioners with stories about his meetings and the important people he had rubbed shoulders with.

The next day, at the office, I suggested that on the next such occasion he spend more time getting to know the guests. I even gave him questions to ask about their lives. But evening two turned out to be a replay of the first—with many of the exact same stories! The people felt they knew *him* better, but he learned nothing about any of them.

Another replay of the above, and another attempt on my part to reverse the flow of the conversation, again proved abortive. I believe that was the first time I realized ministers have been trained to talk, which does not equal knowing how to listen! Like the man who knew very little about fixing toilets, ministers don't know much about asking questions and then paying close attention to what people have to say. If a minister has not learned the skill of sincere listening, which comes on the heels of asking good questions, he or she will be hard-pressed to find out about someone else's world. If they don't develop the capacity to step outside their own concerns and deeply into others, they will not truly understand how to lead their congregation from the "whats" to the "how-tos."

One Last Thought

"Before you go outside this Saturday, buster, you need to clean your room!" Your words have a certain bite to them, so your fourth-grader knows you mean what you're telling him.

But does your boy know how to pull off what you're expecting? Is what you have in mind little more than picking a few things up off the floor, or does it include changing the sheets on his bed as well as vacuuming under it? By the way, has he ever been taught how to properly make a bed?

Maybe ministers aren't the only adults to assume those who listen to them are as learned and as practiced as they are!

Your son is not sophisticated enough to explain his dilemma to you. But in your case, that's not the problem. So every time you hear something in church that challenges you to act in a way that's beyond your experience, you need to say so. No, not during the service … but a gracious letter, or email, or phone call is certainly in order.

"Pastor, I've never given a Sunday School lesson before. I know the church needs new teachers, like you made clear, but quite honestly, the assignment sounds intimidating to me. When and where can I learn more about how to do this?"

If a sermon leaves you clueless as to how to respond to it, you need to explain your situation. Just sitting in your room, feeling guilty and sulking like your son, is not a good option.

Chapter 5

How Long Is It Going to Take?

....

S piritual change can happen quickly. For example, once a seeker understands what becoming a Christian involves, the actual act of inviting the Spirit of Jesus to enter a life can take place in a minute or so. That's why preachers often say, "You can experience new life in Christ before you leave this building."

Other aspects of growing in the Lord, however, take longer. Let me illustrate from my personal walk of faith. I am a recovering workaholic. I recall some years back sharing this on our national radio program *The Chapel of the Air*. A listener wrote in and said it was brave of me to admit publicly that I was a recovering *alcoholic*, and that she would be sure to pray for me.

I informed her that she had misunderstood. Then I also explained that it was as difficult for me to say "no" to work as it is for an alcoholic to pass up the bottle. My battle was just a different kind of addiction.

Being workaholic hurt me because at its root, workaholism is idolatry. I loved my busyness more than the One I was supposedly so busy for. My sin also hurt those closest to me, as alcoholism invariably does as well. "So yes," I wrote back to the listener, "even though the problem is different from what you originally thought, please do pray for me."

I have vivid memories of the occasion in my life when, after years of living in denial, everything became crystal-clear and I knew things had to change. There was an overwhelming conviction of sin. Many tears were shed. I confessed the evil and begged for divine forgiveness. The matter was made right with God that night, but it still took 3 or 4 years before I actually began saying to anyone, "I'm a *recovering* workaholic."

During that time, a long series of adjustments began to change my life and habits. It was almost like slowly unwinding the strong coils of a monstrous snake that was suffocating me. I began to be stripped of the jobs I loved, and I was reluctant to see them go. This period in my life was incredibly difficult, but also phenomenally freeing. My point is that not all spiritual success comes about instantaneously.

This observation is critical. Truth be told, a great deal of spiritual growth takes longer than most people suspect. You don't become a master-handler of God's Word in a month or two. Proficiency at prayer is not learned in a week. Ultimate victory over subtle sins is often meticulously slow. Learning to be a "bold witness for Jesus" requires different amounts of time for different people. Some will catch on quickly; others might never find talking about the Lord all that natural.

I make these comments because ministers have a tendency to think people change spiritually much faster than is normally the case. Preaching for one sermon on being bold witnesses probably won't accomplish much. "But that's all the time I can give that topic," protests a minister doing a series on Acts. "Next Sunday I have to move on to chapter 3, which is about Peter healing the crippled beggar at the gate called Beautiful." Who would imagine that preaching through a book study might actually be counterproductive when life change becomes the bottom line?

Let's go back to the Old Testament passage we've looked at several times. Psalm 1 is about the individual who wants to experience God's blessings. Such a person should seek to get advice about living from the right source, not from questionable ones. You remember this, right?

That good source is God's Word (v. 2, *"But his delight is in the law of the LORD, and on his law he meditates day and night"*). Now, how many Sunday sermons will it take on the topic of meditating on the Word before a significant number of people understand AND begin to live out what is being preached? That is, how long will it be before many folks in the congregation actually begin to practice meditating on Scripture?

1 Sunday	3 Sundays
2 Sundays	More than 3 Sundays

What about mastering how-tos related to showing greater discernment regarding input received from questionable sources such as television, movies, books, magazines, etc? How long before keen insight starts marking people's lives in these areas?

1 Sunday	3 Sundays
2 Sundays	More than 3 Sundays

Add up your two answers, then answer this next question. How many Sundays will the typical minister preach on Psalm 1? You know the answer. It's one and done!

Does this mean a congregation needs to hear four to eight sermons in a row on a short text like Psalm 1?

Not necessarily. If more time is needed to teach certain lessons, there are many related passages that can be referenced. It's just that some mental work should go into thinking through what's a reasonable amount of time to spend before a minister can expect people to not only understand but also begin to live out the truth being presented. Unfortunately, the time issue is seldom addressed in sermon planning or preaching.

Let's review the four simple sermon questions that listeners should be able to answer following any sermon they hear:

1. What was the subject?
2. What was the response called for?
3. What was the how-to?
4. What was the how-long?

If, at the end of a message, few listeners can come up with these answers, is it any wonder that on Monday they can't remember what the minister said on Sunday?

This time factor (the how-long) relates not only to individual sermons but also to sermon series. To illustrate this, let's say your pastor decides to preach some messages based on Paul's letter to the Galatians. The traditional approach would be to start with chapter 1, verse 1 and divide the book into sequential sections that can be covered reasonably in the course of a sermon. You could take a quick look at the book's six chapters and estimate about how many sermons that would require.

The alternative approach I suggest is to first determine the subject of Paul's letter. Most scholars agree that Galatians is about the freedom believers have in Christ. This is in contrast to trying to live by the Old Testament law, as certain Jewish leaders were demanding of early Gentile converts. Of course, this new freedom in Christ is not to be confused with license to live any way one pleases. Instead, what Paul writes about is *responsible freedom.*

In his letter about responsible freedom, the response the apostle hopes and prays to see among his friends in the church at Galatia is that Christians be *"led by the Holy Spirit,"* or *"live by the Spirit,"* *"keep in step with the Spirit,"* *"sow to the Spirit,"* etc. Paul uses a number of phrases that all refer to the same concept.

Does the average Christian today know how to do this—how to live by the Spirit? Most likely the answer is no. If the pastor believes the average Christian in the pew knows how to *"live by the Spirit,"* then he only needs one sermon to cover this territory. But I suspect I need more help than a one-time sermon, and I think you probably do too.

Rather than spell out some appropriate how-tos, allow me to ask again: How long will it take to teach those listening to the series how to live by the Spirit? Can this be done in one Sunday? Unlikely. Two Sundays? Probably not. It will take at least six to eight Sundays to accomplish such a task.

Fine. Then that's about how long it'll take to teach what Galatians is about. Meeting this bottom-line concern—how long will it take for listeners to begin learning to live by the Spirit—has little to do with how many pages, chapters, sentences or words are in the epistle. To bring Paul's words alive for this generation will be determined, more than anything else, by the subject, response, how-tos, and by how long it takes to see that these truths are built into people's lives. More specifically, how many Sundays will it take before those hearing the Galatians series start to be more and more sensitive to the promptings of the Holy Spirit and thus learn to live in *responsible freedom*? Make sense?

Sometimes the desired response of a long section of Scripture can be incorporated into people's lives in a relatively brief period of time, whereas a shorter passage takes more time to penetrate our thought patterns and life habits. Remember Psalm 1?

How discouraging to listen to months of preaching on a given section of Scripture, and in the end have no idea what the bottom line is and how it should mark your life. I contend that you deserve to know about how much time it should take you, an average Christian, to start putting into practice the response being called for.

Time is a huge influence in our culture, but it's not often factored into sermon preparation. When school or the workday ends, we're ready to head home pronto! If friends say they'll meet you at the mall at 7:00, you expect them to be there and on time. If you hire a tutor to teach you Spanish, you want to know how long it'll be before you can start to speak it. Similarly, you need, as does your minister, to be realistic about the length of time it will take for your life to change as a result of preaching. Why is it the element of time has been largely forgotten when it comes to sermons and their impact?

Oh, I agree that congregations no longer allow preachers to just talk on and on. Ministers have less time than their earlier-generation counterparts to say what it is they want. But what I'm asking is, when will congregations start demanding, "Pastor, what specifically do you expect of me? And how much time do I have to start living this way?"

Here's the kind of announcement I'd like to see in a church bulletin:

Next Sunday, Pastor _____ will begin a series of sermons based on Paul's letter to the Galatians. We will spend about two months in this study. During that time, he/she fully expects you to master the skill of keeping in step with the Spirit (Galatians 5:25). Come prepared to learn how to do this and also to start experiencing the excitement of Freedom in Christ, or Responsible Freedom, which is the theme of the book.

We also live in a quick-fix culture. This influence insidiously slides into sermon preparation. Does the preacher, in his sermon, unrealistically expect instant results or change? Are only superficial responses or suggestions given? Does the sermon fail to establish meaningful spiritual disciplines that will require long-range commitment and determined effort? In preaching, these are all examples of quick-fix "shortcuts" that don't actually help and in fact can also create bad listening habits. How long will it take before this spiritual growth becomes a practice (a sustained and effective habit) in your life? Grappling with that essential question will alter the realities of sermon preparation.

If Christians don't take their faith all that seriously, it could be because their leaders aren't pushing them all that hard. Jesus knew He had a little over three years to prepare His followers for when He would be gone. From the Scriptures we know He keenly felt the pressure of this time running out on Him.

The attitude one picks up in all too many American churches is that we have all the time in the world. And this mindset marks both the pulpit and the pew: *Why worry all that much about an invisible, imaginary "black hole"?* Listen to me carefully: We do *not* have all the time in the world. If we expect the Church to once again be a powerful force in this society, that attitude needs to change to one of urgency— and the sooner the better!

One Last Thought

Are you time-conscious? Most Americans are.

Some say, "Time is money." Others lament, "There's never enough time in the day to get everything done."

When thinking about spiritual-growth possibilities, more often than not, your time commitment is one of the important considerations.

- Should I be spending more time in the word?
- How much time should a volunteer teacher plan on when preparing a Sunday School lesson?

• As a new Christian, what's a recommended amount of time to target each day for prayer?

Is it wrong to expect definitive answers to questions like these? Of course not.

Being expected to respond to challenging sermons that don't include time considerations is a little like being asked to sign loan papers without clearly spelled-out financial terms. "It's going to cost you this much per month for 48 months."

People skilled at budgeting their time are the ones who tend to get a lot done. And yes, you can figure out time factors on your own. However, it's to your advantage to hear what the music minister thinks it's going to take, time-wise, for you to start using your musical gifts in the choir, or what the youth pastor estimates being a teen sponsor involves in terms of hours per week, or what the preaching pastor has in mind when challenging everyone in the congregation to get involved in small groups.

You deserve to know without always having to ask.

Chapter 6

Becoming Your Pastor's Supportive Friend

....

A quick way some congregations are supposedly solving the Black Hole problem of poor sermon retention is by exchanging ministers for videos. As a Sunday pulpit replacement, they merely play a video or get a live feed from the service of some well-known preacher. Just down the road from our West Chicago home, a Willow Creek satellite church fills the auditorium of a nearby Christian high school, where the congregation enjoys the excellent communication skills of the preaching staff from the mother church in Barrington. I'm told this methodology works quite well and is less expensive than looking for and hiring a gifted replacement candidate.

Maybe churches' next move will be to solve their less-than-the-best soloist problem by simply playing music by popular artists. Eventually a church could even subscribe to a "Great Scripture Reader" series. The "Finest Pastoral Prayers" could be on audiotape rather than video, and therefore less expensive because everyone's eyes should be closed when it's played.

But before rushing to adopt such solutions, first the sermons of many "big-name" preachers should be carefully analyzed. Often when I hear supposedly "incredibly dynamic" speakers, I can't glean much more than the basic subject. Maybe the appeal of these "dynamic" personalities is really just that they choose intriguing topics, use fascinating personal illustrations, and speak enthusiastically. Under closer scrutiny, there is often no clear response articulated, hardly ever any how-tos, and there is little consideration of how long individuals will need to incorporate the spiritual-growth concepts mentioned. I fear that certain "great" preachers downloaded into churches will not solve the problem of the Sermon-Sucking Black Hole.

Take away the illustrations, the many verses quoted, and the abundant energy, and sadly, what's preached often turns out to be little more than platitudes. Here's an example of such an empty message and how I, as a listener, would tend to respond to it.

Preacher: "Does trouble make up a big part of your life? That's what the Holy Spirit has laid on my heart to talk about."

Me (thinking): *I'm beginning to get encouraged. Good topic. What's next?*

Preacher: "I'm here to tell you that God is bigger than any problem you have!"

Me: *Agreed.*

Preacher: "Here's why He's bigger. Number one, God is all-powerful. Number two, God is all-knowing. And number three, God is faithful."

Me: *What a letdown. Could have preached those three points in a minute or two without all the amplification, and everyone would have said, "We already know that!"*

Preacher: "Let me see the hands of those who would like to turn your problems over to an all-powerful, all-knowing, faithful God this very night!"

Me (now frustrated): *Give me a break. Who wouldn't like to do that? But **how?***

Preacher: "I see hands everywhere—a vast sea of hands. Thank you, Jesus."

Me: *I can't believe this. What does he think actually has happened here?*

Granted, some preachers' verbal skills are outstanding—especially if inspiration is what turns your crank. But the big question is whether or not what these preachers say results in Christ-like behavior on the part of those who listen. Sometimes it does. But all too often, I'm afraid, it doesn't.

I don't know how many books have been written for ministers to help them become better preachers, but there are hundreds. If you want to borrow a couple, I have more than a few in my library.

When I decided to write this little book, I made a conscious choice to target listeners more than speakers. That's because I'm convinced that today's sermon-related problems will never be solved without your help.

I sincerely doubt your pastor or priest has requested your input in sermon- or service-planning. You predict that if you were to make such an offer, it would likely be politely turned down—right? Like everyone else, ministers aren't all that excited about having untrained laypeople evaluate their work.

I've seen my 4 simple questions transform the preaching of many less-than-exceptional preachers, but before you employ these questions to work on behalf of your church, let's consider how to establish credibility with your pastor.

First, a fast review. As you are reading this book, ask yourself, *"What is its subject?"* (How about, "Is there a Sermon-Sucking Black Hole at my church?")

*What's the **desired response** of this exercise?* We want better retention of what's being preached. If attendees can't recall what was said, how are lives going to change?

*What about the **how-long**?* Right up front it will be helpful to recognize that it's going to take not days and weeks, but months and probably years to solve this problem.

*Now back to the **how-to.*** Here's the hard part. Let's start with establishing credibility. If you as a layperson don't practice the following suggestions, authenticity won't accompany your sincere concerns. In my work with pastors, I know how much they agonize over being good handlers of the Word in the pulpit. That unrelenting schedule of having something significant to say every seven days is daunting to most of them. And their sermon-preparation time is often interrupted by crises in the lives of their people. Even when they feel weary or sick or discouraged, their role demands they have something profitable to say, Sunday after Sunday, 52 weeks a year, year after year. Your concern about ineffective sermons must clearly come from a heart of compassion for the preachers. Here are a few suggestions that will help.

Pray for Your Pastor Consistently

I don't necessarily mean spending long periods of time doing this. But every day you should make it a point to uphold your pastor in prayer. Maybe it's as you bow your head at lunch during the workweek, or before falling asleep in the evening, while driving to church for a service, riding the train, whenever. But if you say to your minister, "I'm praying for you," *you want it to be the truth.* If it's not the truth, please don't say it.

You can pray about key congregational relationships the pastor has; for his/her spouse and children; any church struggles you are aware of; about sermon preparation, of course; protection; wisdom; potential areas of temptation; for continued spiritual growth; problem personalities in the congregation; and so on. Pray so consistently that your pastor's name just pops up regularly in your mind.

Love Your Pastor as Jesus Does

Try to see your pastor through Jesus' eyes. What prompted the Lord to choose this person to be one He called to represent Him in this way? Agree with Jesus that He made a good choice.

All the original Twelve were flawed in one way or another, but Jesus loved each of them despite their failings. Does our Lord feel that way about your minister as well? Then do your best to act toward him or her the way you believe Christ would were He a visible part of the congregation. Some people are naturally gifted at this; others need to learn by example.

Pray for your pastor consistently, and love your pastor as Jesus does. These are not just nice devotional thoughts you say "amen" to and then forget. They are attitudes and actions that need to mark your life, if you have any thoughts whatsoever of someday helping defeat the sinister force of the wide-mouthed, invisible Black Hole.

Take Notes During Your Pastor's Sermons

I believe people who take notes listen more closely than those who don't. They can also recall what was said much more quickly than a casual listener can.

Note-taking conveys a mindset of expecting to receive something of worth. Not doing so projects an attitude of not expecting to hear much of value. Writing down what you hear should also quickly clarify whether the 4 simple questions have been covered. Even if they haven't been, you'll probably be able to answer some of them on your own.

Note-takers have a valuable reference to go to if the opportunity ever comes to talk through sermons with a pastor. Those who must rely exclusively on their memory will find it generally isn't all that reliable.

It's common for churches nowadays to provide a sheet in the Sunday bulletin for taking notes. My opinion is that bringing a small notebook with your Bible to church is the best way to keep everything orderly and in one place.

Become a Good Listener

In her excellent book *The Great American Sermon Survey*, Dr. Lori Carrell, using her background and experience as a professor of communication, insists that the sermon event is not a one-sided oral experience. Indeed, she teaches that preachers and listeners co-create meaning together; they are actually partners in preaching. One of the ways this occurs is to assume the responsibility incumbent on the hearer to become a good listener.

After all, Dr. Carrell insists, if you are now 40 years old, that means you will listen to approximately 35 more years of preaching. This figure times 50 Sundays a year (we all get sick or skip church every now and then) equals 1750 sermons times 20 minutes (we'll make this sermon length an average). Being a bad listener means you are probably going to waste 35,000 minutes of the rest of your life.

Carrell divides listening competency into five areas: attending, comprehending, remembering, evaluating and responding. That's quite a task for the listener in the pew, but unless we choose to be active listeners, we cannot claim the right to be constructive participants in changing the sermon status-quo.

Attending means you come prepared to listen to the sermon, that you not let your mind develop the habit of daydreaming, recipe-gathering, solving life's various dilemmas or whatever it is that tempts you to become mentally vacant when the sermon is preached.

Comprehending means you work intentionally with the 4 sermon-evaluation questions we've been developing. If the pastor has not answered these questions in the preaching event, see if you can work with the Scripture yourself, as you sit in the worship space. What is the passage calling for you to do? What would be a practical how-to that would help put this response in place in your life? How long is it going to take?

Remembering means finding ways to get past the Sermon-Sucking Black Hole in the parking lot and take the meaning of the message into Monday. Can you go over your notes in your notebook early the next morning? Ask the Holy Spirit, "What is it You want me to do with this word?"

Evaluating means you need to analyze the message. Is what was said really true? Do you agree or not? Is the speaker's logic faulty? Could the concept have been more clearly expressed? This may seem like a negative activity, but without evaluation going on in the intellects God has given us, we commit that unpardonable of listener sins: We become passive hearers, all but tossing the spiritual information we've received into the Black Hole as we exit the service.

Responding is the acid test of whether a sermon is effective or not. Are we going to do anything specific with what we've heard? Are we going to lean toward the response called for in the Scripture (and hopefully in the sermon)? Train yourself to consider this question carefully; talk about it with your family and friends.

Compliment Your Pastor Whenever Possible
There are many reasons to do this, not the least being that it's probably deserved. All ministers have strengths as well as weaknesses. They

generally hear enough about the latter and not that much about the former. Some things you might say are:

"Your sermon about _____ challenged me to make some major changes in my week."

"Your love of God's Word is obvious and so infectious."

"During your pastoral prayers, I can almost picture Jesus giving you His full attention."

"It seems like you're always smiling. I like that."

"Thank you for taking an active interest in our children's lives."

What I'm suggesting is not to be mistaken for flattery. Your remarks need to be genuine. Not all that many people, however, are comfortable affirming those in positions of spiritual leadership. Why not determine to become someone who is?

A note of thanks, an email, or a short phone call saying "your message on Sunday was great" will go a long way toward ensuring that your thoughts in a future brainstorm session are heard and appreciated. Constructive criticism is always more easily received when it comes from a known supporter.

Offer Help When Your Pastor Seems Ready

Most ministers experienced a time of sermon evaluation during their seminary training. They were critiqued on both content and style of delivery. They went through with the assignment because they had to. It wasn't something most of them requested.

I'm not suggesting anything close to that same kind of exercise when pastors ask for input from the congregation. This is not like a professor grading a student. Rather, it's part of the role of becoming an active listener—the people who listen to sermons Sunday after Sunday revealing what is most helpful to them and what is not. Restated, it's a loving church family attempting to function in the best way possible for the good of all.

Once it's realized how beneficial such a process can be, ministers value it highly. But without that understanding of its potential value, listener feedback can be viewed as threatening or even demeaning. So your thoughtful, loving input is never to be dumped on a pastor "ready or not."

Every so often peers seek out my personal opinion. "What did you think of the service (or even the sermon)?" they'll ask. I usually reply, "I'll make a few observations in writing, if you'd like." Sometimes the response is a quick, "Oh, no, don't go to that trouble." So I don't. My reason is that unsought advice is seldom well-received.

I've also had men and women of the cloth who respect and trust me respond differently: "I'd be honored and grateful if you would take the time to do that." Some later informed me they kept and prized what I wrote to them.

Anyway, I'm obviously suggesting a different solution than replacing a less-than-spellbinding pastor with a preacher on video. My alternative approach involves, for now, positioning yourself as a supportive friend who prays consistently for your minister. Attempt to always show your pastor the love Jesus would were He in the congregation. Because of a conviction regarding the importance of preaching, take notes during each sermon. Train yourself to become an active and responsive listener. Then, as an affirming person, be always ready and willing to offer your help when it's wanted and called for.

One Last Thought

Can you tell when somebody is supportive and on your team?

Most of the time we think we know who our true friends are. Haven't we logged a lot of miles together? We feel safe even when these people confront us about something. Occasionally someone fools us, but not often.

Ministers are like everyone else. They sense who is on their team. These are the people they are most comfortable being around. A trust factor has been built over a period of time.

The guidelines in this chapter should help in this regard. They aren't really all that complicated. For example, praying for your pastor is just a given. It's hard to have a bad attitude about someone you've been interceding for regularly, especially if you have been asking the Lord to bring good into this person's life.

When was the last time you went out of your way to let your minister know that you pray regularly for him or her? And are you looking for ways to make positive comments to your pastor whenever possible? As simple as these suggestions sound, they communicate clearly that you don't ever want to be classified among the indifferent or the negative in the church.

Good friendships aren't the result of passive behavior. Becoming someone your pastor sees as a supporter requires some effort on your part.

Chapter 7

The "Sunday Search" Game

···

Recently I went out of my way to tell a minister how meaningful his sermon was. His response surprised me. "Thank you so much. You encourage me more than you realize. Lately it seems all I've heard about my preaching have been complaints."

What would account for such strikingly different feedback? I'm convinced that much of it depends on the worship attitude one brings to a service. Can I share a good habit that's marked my life for some decades now?

When I go to church, it's my practice to play a simple game I created called the "Sunday Search." In one sense, I don't like using the word "game" because what I do is not frivolous to me. Then again, "game" captures the sense of delight and excitement this routine affords me. My "Sunday Search" begins with looking for how God might speak TO me during the morning.

This can happen in any number of ways. The most obvious would be during the sermon. Maybe it's my conscience nudging me. Sometimes I will experience a strong sense of conviction. Occasionally it's a special insight I gain that helps me figure out the answer to a problem I've been wrestling with. But I'm determined not to be a passive listener. Throughout the entire service my mind is actively searching for how God might want to speak TO me.

Music is another common means through which I sense a message from the Lord. As I search for what He might want to say to me, it could be He uses the words of a hymn to convey His thoughts. I'm also aware the Lord regularly speaks to people through a choral selection or a solo someone sings. At the same time, songs can be little more than religious entertainment if you aren't honestly listening for how God might speak to you.

I personally pay extra-close attention when the Scriptures are read. Sometimes I even close my eyes to block out distractions and imagine the human writers like Moses, David, Isaiah, John or Paul reading the words aloud while writing under the influence of the Holy Spirit. I find God's Word to be very powerful when I concentrate on what's being read and open myself to God speaking TO me in this fashion.

Over the years, I've found it's not uncommon to hear God's voice in unexpected ways. I recall inviting a couple to church with us one Sunday. I assumed their two kids would be happy in the children's-church program. Their 7-year-old daughter was, but not their 5-year-old son. Would you believe he sat through the adult service and hardly moved? But when it was time for the Lord's Table, he started to get restless. So I plunked him on my lap and started to rub his back. (I didn't raise four kids of my own without learning a trick or two.) Totally contented once again, soon this little fellow looked at me as if to say, "You have to be one of the nicest men in the whole world." Unfortunately, he couldn't express himself like he wanted, because by now the congregation was singing as the elements were being served. So he said nothing and just reveled in his good fortune. Now the deacons carried their trays back to the front. The singing stopped as our minister served these men and prepared to have us partake together. But for my new young friend, the relative silence was his chance to finally say what he wanted to. In a voice I'd call a stage whisper—meaning his words could be heard two or three pews in all directions—he said, very clearly for a 5-year-old, "You … you weigh more than you should, don't you?" On the way home, my wife, Karen, asked with a sly smile, "Did the Lord have a special word just for you this morning, sweetheart?"

The truth is that God does sometimes speak to us at church, even through the comments of others before or after the service. Has anyone ever said to you, like they have to me, "I believe Jesus wants me to tell you that…"? Maybe the approach in your case was less direct. But suppose you expressed to God how lonely you've been feeling. Then one Sunday someone asked, "How would you like to join a few of us for lunch today?" And could you believe this was God's way of saying, "I heard your prayer, and this is how I'm answering it."

Does Christ speak clearly to me every Sunday? No, not always. But it happens far more often than you might think. I'm convinced the problem is not so much one of Him being silent as it is that most people don't come to church prepared to hear Him speak.

Part two of this three-part "Sunday Search" "game" is not only to look for ways God speaks TO me, but also THROUGH me—TO and THROUGH. That's easy enough to remember on a Sunday morning. How can Jesus reach out to someone else THROUGH me?

Again, it's not that the living Christ doesn't want to minister when the church body is gathered. It's just that there aren't many who open themselves to allowing Him to do mini-miracles THROUGH them.

For example, many in the church are hurting because they lack money. I'm not talking about great sums, but usually just enough to buy necessities. It's too bad that fellow believers with more than they need seldom say to the Lord, "I have an extra $20 in my pocket this morning. If I hear someone is lacking, I'll give this to them in Your name, Lord. If I'm not aware of any needs, fine. But just know that I'm waiting for You to kind of tap me on the shoulder and say, 'Act now. Be an answer to someone's prayer on my behalf.'"

One Sunday, having said such a prayer, I remember being surprised to see a college student standing at the back of the church. "What's the deal?" I asked when I caught up to him. "Are you on break or something?" "No," he responded, "I just got up early this morning and was lonely for our church, so I drove the 40 miles to be here." Then he laughed and said, "Hoping I'll make it back on the gas I have." It was an innocent comment on his part, but for me it was like the Lord said, "That was your cue. Out with the twenty and give it to him." "Oh," I said, "this is for you." The young man was surprised and deeply touched that the Lord had answered his prayer. The truth is, I had just experienced the excitement of answered prayer as well!

In a similar way, the Lord can minister THROUGH you to others by means of hospitality. Fix a brunch or lunch and tell the Lord, "This is ready for someone, but I'm not sure who. I'm going to church today expecting You to prompt me when it's the right time to extend an invitation."

Buy a bag of groceries on Saturday and have it in your car when you go to church. Believe there's a family in need, and you just have to prayerfully give the Lord a chance to somehow network who that party is so He can minister THROUGH you.

Lots of people carry pain with them to church. Sometimes all they need is someone to listen to them talk. Tell the Lord some Sunday that your ears are His if He wants them to patiently hear a fellow worshiper talk through their grief. Feel honored when God takes you up on your offer. It's another way He can minister THROUGH you.

God can obviously speak THROUGH you as you sing or teach or pray or usher. "Jesus, I'm reading the Scripture during the morning service. But beyond my human skills, I need You to minister to others THROUGH me. Please do that." This should be a regular prayer of those in public ministries. And it's wonderful to be affirmed by comments like, "God really spoke to my heart as you were praying in today's service." But that experience should be known by many who attend church, not just the few in public ministries. Christ can speak THROUGH you to others practically every Sunday if you give Him the opportunity.

For example, when you hear that someone is hurting, don't just say, "I'll be praying for you," as affirming as that might be. Usually it's appropriate to pray for the person right then and there. If you need to, find a quiet place to reach out in this way.

Sharing a verse from Scripture or spiritual wisdom should be a natural Sunday practice for many believers. In too many settings it's not.

Acts of kindness from little children have been known to melt hearts about as fast as anything. I have a grade-school-age granddaughter who is great at giving hugs to people. I too am learning how meaningful this can be, and in the process have come to realize how often Jesus ministered to people through touch.

How will God minister TO me and THROUGH me?—these are two questions that bring a great sense of delight to my worship experience. I believe they can do the same to yours.

One last element: Every Sunday, there needs to be a time to debrief what has been experienced. That is, I need a chance to TALK ABOUT what happened. My "Sunday Search" results are not to remain private. Verbally revealing your Sunday experience to another will often solidify that experience for yourself, deepen it in your soul. Perhaps more remarkably, there is a rich and edifying sharing that occurs between members of the Body of Christ. I get to hear how a certain part of the service or sermon (which perhaps didn't stand out to me) has moved or challenged someone I love. This teaches me respect for the work of the Holy Spirit and the differences that exist between us all. In addition, talking about the sermon and service with each other often completes the worship experience and the sermon event. Our conversation takes us along paths that we hadn't the time to walk during the service.

Often Karen and I TALK ABOUT our TOs and THROUGHs on the way home in the car. Sometimes we stop for lunch and share our discoveries. When the kids were still around, dinner at the dining-room table was the most common place for going over what happened. If one of our four children had nothing to contribute to the discussion, that son or daughter wasn't faulted. The excitement of those who did was a natural incentive to encourage better participation the next week.

Playing the *Sunday Search* game has convinced me I have more to bring to the worship setting than I once thought. Yes, my minister plays a major role in what takes place. But so do I. The problem of the Black Hole is not solely the clergy's responsibility. If others consistently hear from God and for some reason I seldom do, I need to look at myself before I start blaming someone else.

I believe if you follow these three simple T's of TO, THROUGH, and TALK ABOUT, even if the services you attend don't change much, the living Christ will become more real to you through playing this spiritual "game" (you can also call it a spiritual practice).

Of course, as the popularity of this activity grows in your congregation, the expectancy level heightens as well. "Did Christ speak TO you this morning?" my pastor asked me following the service a few Sundays back.

"He sure did!" I responded. He smiled and seemed relieved. I felt perhaps I had put unfair pressure on him. He's an excellent preacher. But it is not his responsibility to see to it that the miracle of the Church of the living God is experienced each Sunday in my life. I am as integral to that mystery as he is.

One Last Thought

This is one of my favorite chapters. I feel that way because I know the effectiveness of the "Sunday Search" game.

As someone who normally sits with the congregation, I've been on this search for some three decades now. One of my surprising discoveries during this extended time period is that God can still speak quite clearly TO ME, even when the person preaching fails to answer any of the four key questions I so carefully laid out earlier.

When a given service could be characterized as anything but seamless, because it appears to go in a dozen different directions, God can still speak THROUGH ME to someone else.

Whether the morning in church was fantastic or not much to write home about, it's always to my advantage to TALK ABOUT what took place. And the way the "Sunday Search" is arranged, the onus is on me and God more than on anyone or anything else to find meaning in what happened. Since everyone pretty much knows how God is reputed to take care of His responsibilities, guess who needs to make sure he's on top of what he's searching for?

Don't get me wrong—the Sermon-Sucking Black Hole is real. If I didn't believe that, I wouldn't have written a book about it! But I also know it takes more than passive church attendance to ensure a Sunday encounter with the living God. That's where playing this weekly game becomes so beneficial.

Chapter 8

Soliciting Listener Input

···

Saturday mornings when running errands, I often switch on the car radio for Click and Clack, the Tappet Brothers. These two have the uncanny knack of making me feel like I can actually understand what they are talking about, when in reality I know practically nothing about autos or their repairs.

Car Talk is the name of their incredibly popular hour-long show on National Public Radio. Rather than speak a technical language, the two hosts, Tom and Ray Magliozzi, make me laugh out loud while they casually discuss cars in a manner that everyone can enjoy. What I really like is that those who call in with questions are never treated as dummies. Also, the brothers regularly poke fun at their own abilities, even though it's obvious they are experts in their field.

I picture myself in a similar role as I write about sermons. My attempt is not to reduce the sublime to the ridiculous, but just to a level that allows common folk to get involved in the discussion. And when using that word *common*, I am fully aware that many of you who read my thoughts are remarkably knowledgeable about farming, teaching, selling, coaching, flying, accounting, gardening, printing, cooking, engineering, acting, banking, governing, painting, repairing, sailing, and a thousand other amazing skills. It's just that preaching is not a topic you have explored that much. But to me, it's important that all of you individuals demonstrate a keen interest, because, again, you are the ones who are in the best position to judge the real effectiveness of sermons.

You no doubt noticed my 4 questions purposely avoid words like *hermeneutics*, *exegesis* and *exposition*. Such terms only confuse the uninitiated, just as a few too many *carburetors*, *manifolds* and *camshafts* would make me feel the car talk had just gone over my head. When a fresh breeze starts to blow in people's minds, I don't want a window slammed shut because words are too technical for the average person to understand.

I believe that, though elementary, the four simple questions discussed in the previous chapters—*subject, response, how to, how long*—get at the heart of what good preaching is all about. They are remarkably simple, yet incredibly profound. When honored, they greatly enhance communication. They also define the discussion so it doesn't fragment and go in a thousand different directions.

When it's obvious a message has clearly addressed these four matters, take a moment to celebrate before you start thinking how it could have been stronger. Where a sermon misses the mark, use the four simple questions to offer constructive help for future presentations and to hopefully keep the discussion from degenerating into a "roast the preacher" session. I believe the day will come when ministers and congregants, in an effort to enhance communication, regularly sit together and discuss what was preached.

When I was a senior minister, I accomplished this every Sunday in what was called the Pastor's Class. Whoever wanted to was welcome to stay and be part of a group of ten or twelve who talked about what they heard. If there were more people, we broke into smaller groups, which other staff members were prepared to lead.

I always started by asking people in the circle to give their names and then put into a sentence what they thought I was saying. I recall one morning when I preached on a tough section from Romans. I had wrestled all week with the passage and wasn't all that pleased with my message. The summaries from the group went in all different directions. This was quite a contrast to the single focus I usually heard by way of feedback. Finally one gentleman looked at me and said rather innocently, "I'm really struggling, Pastor. Why don't you put into a sentence for us what it is you were trying to say." I knew I was in trouble, because I wasn't entirely sure *I* could!

That "Black Hole" experience proved a turning point in my ministry. From that embarrassing morning on, I have always been ready to reply to anyone questioning me:

"My subject was _____. The response being called for was _____. Here's how I felt people could pull that off: _____. And how long it should take, I would estimate to be _____."

An even better strategy for me was discussing with people in the congregation my sermons while they were still being formed. Every week, my secretary would send out postcards to different members of the church, inviting them to our home on Tuesday evening for a two-hour brainstorming session about the message two Sundays ahead. Usually between four and ten people would show up.

It was during these sessions that I learned the importance of those four questions. I would begin our time with prayer and some gathering chitchat. Then I would say, "(1) This is the working subject for my sermon. Is it relevant to where you are? (2) Here's the response the passage calls for. Have I worded it in a way that's appropriate for where our people are coming from? (3) What do you think of these ideas regarding how-tos? (4) Does my estimated timeline make sense?"

Often we differed. Yet regularly I found lay input invaluable. Without a doubt, these weekly sessions over ten years radicalized my preaching approach. I often found myself being told to slow down: I was expecting too much in my sermons. The people were being challenged too fast and too frequently. What was elementary to me, they considered advanced. Praying was more difficult than I made it sound. The Bible wasn't nearly as interesting to them as it appeared to be to me. I regularly heard, "How nice it must be to not have to work a regular job and to concentrate only on spiritual things!"

We all have our misconceptions of what "the other guy's" life must be like. Ministers certainly do. I know I did. But over time I came to understand and trust this input. It's not that we always saw eye-to-eye, but these men and women who came to help certainly knew better than I did how my sermon affected their worlds.

Often during the next week and a half someone in the group would phone with an illustration from their area of interest or field of expertise. Early on in the process I discovered these people were my biggest supporters on the Sunday "their" sermon was preached. "Been praying for you, Pastor," I was told more than once. By being open to their input I had earned their support and respect. We were in this together!

I recall during those years being interviewed by a reporter for a Christian magazine on the subject of preaching. "Do you have a favorite commentary?" he asked. Commentaries are reference books ministers regularly turn to when preparing sermons. All kinds are available, including many classics by well-known names from the past, like Martin Luther and Matthew Henry. Quite a few modern-day pulpiteers have been published this way as well.

"Yes," I replied, "I prefer Elliott, Dutter, Reiter, and DeBoer." These names were all new to my interviewer, so he asked if they were classic or more-contemporary writers. "Modern," I said, "though they haven't actually published anything. But time and again I find their insights right on target." I was referring, of course, to the church members who consistently volunteered to help in my sermon- and service-planning. I discovered my laypeople were the best living commentaries available. Their wisdom, knowledge and practical understanding were vast, untapped resources needing to be accessed.

Meeting with a small group of supportive people is highly stimulating. Too many ministers know all too well what it's like to sit alone at their desk for a long morning or afternoon, trying to set a direction for the next sermon. Sometimes they end up back where they started and see the time as wasted. Having live people present tends to force the issue. If pastors don't have any fresh ideas, laypeople have any number of them!

That's where having predetermined boundaries is so important. "Listen, we're trying first to come up with a subject that will grab people's attention. But it has to be consistent with what our assigned passage is saying." Or, if the approach is topical rather than textual, "This has to be a theme that's found in Scripture without manipulating what the Bible teaches." If clear direction like this isn't established, a lively discussion on spiritual matters can go just about anywhere. I found it to everyone's benefit to always rely on the four simple questions as my agenda.

When I moved from the pastorate to become part of a radio outreach, I lost my pool of people to draw upon. Instead of preaching each Sunday, I was now responsible for six broadcasts a week. The messages were shorter (about 12 minutes), but I soon found that the less time you have to say something, the more carefully your message has to be crafted. Planning enough brainstorming sessions to cover this new kind of schedule was out of the question.

We had a staff of about 50, however. Now my co-workers became a huge source of support. I would call a man in the warehouse to get his response to a given how-to. The head of the outgoing sales team could always free a few minutes to share her thoughts about where this or that broadcast script was headed. Interns from various schools felt honored to be included. Their responses to my invitation were always positive. "Anytime. No, I enjoyed it. Thank you for asking for my ideas."

On top of a daily radio show, television was next added to the schedule, with five new half-hour programs produced every week. (Remember that I have already admitted it was wrong to take on so much.) The four questions served me exceedingly well, clarifying and organizing my thoughts quickly and effectively. So did those who worked with me. Few of them had any training to be a reverend, but they were incredibly helpful when it came to honestly informing me if my content had value. Frankly, I learned to go to the people within my realm of influence before I went to any published commentaries; the people represented exactly those audiences I was speaking to, and their observations were pertinent and invaluable.

Let's go back to *Car Talk* again. Those of you acquainted with this NPR program know that the show always closes with both of the hosts cautioning listeners, "Don't drive like my brother." It's a funny line. After an hour of nationwide advice-giving, these two guys go back to the one thing just about any listener should be able to do—drive— and they both say that you'd be smart not to do it like his brother, the "expert," does.

Too often ministers preach sermons that relate mostly to their worlds. I believe it's time for all of us in ministry to realize the goal is not to try to make congregants into carbon copies of professional ministers. You the layperson don't have to be an expert in a theologian. You don't have to be current with info in the latest periodicals for pastors. You don't have to know the latest thinking on trends in understanding church history. Nor do you need to know the Greek and Hebrew root words.

What you *do* need to know is how to raise your children to be godly followers of Christ, how to be compassionate with that office colleague who is such a pain in the neck, how to make moral decisions when the ethics in your work place are questionable, how to take care of the high-security-prison inmate released into a halfway program and now being sponsored by your church. You need to know how to overcome envy, greed and lust, how to be a Christian friend to the friendless, how to love the unlovable.

"No, don't do it like we do!" Church members aren't to turn into part-time versions of full-time pastors. Rather, simple sermons should be preached that train people to be good Christians in their various unique callings. But all too often, preachers haven't the faintest idea what that looks like. Too many of them are still composing sermons that will receive the approval of their seminary professor and their student colleagues. We need to be asking: What does it mean to be a Christian politician, landlord, nurse, soldier, restaurant owner, recording artist, teacher, ballplayer? The truth is, without a lot of dialoguing, evaluating, brainstorming and advising from these very kinds of individuals, the "experts" really won't know if they're helping much or how to change their approach.

One Last Thought
He was a well-dressed older gentleman who had listened patiently while I shared my thoughts about the value of getting congregational feedback while in the process of preparing sermons. During the discussion time he said, with a slight roll of his eyes, "I just can't imagine any minister wanting someone like me to help write his sermon."

"Actually, I can't either," I responded, "but that's not exactly what I'm calling for. Ultimately your pastor is the one who's going to have to put his sermon together. But in the early stages, when he's finalizing the subject, the response, and the answers to the "how to" and "how long" questions, that's when I think, sir, that hearing your opinion would be extremely helpful. Like how interested are you in this proposed subject?

Would you say his desired response seems fair? Will the "how-tos" he's suggesting work for you? Is the timeline for getting everything done appropriate? What you have to say in response to questions like these should be extremely valuable.

"Granted, there will still be a lot of work to make everything gel when it's preached. But it's like there's an emotional charge to complete the task when you're working on a message you're confident will touch lives in a positive way.

"So, no, he wont expect you to help him write his sermon, but he should be grateful for input that gives him the motivation to get moving on it!"

I thought it was a great answer. I'm not sure what the well-dressed gentleman thought.

Chapter 9

Living a Lie Isn't the Answer

....

A strange memory I retain from my years as a pastor concerns a young man I'll call Harry Marvel. I can't recall how we met, but before long, I became aware of his remarkable skill as an organist. He had ever so many unique stories about playing various instruments in the greater Chicagoland area, mostly in churches and universities. I found it fascinating to hear him compare the good and bad features of these grand instruments.

Harry was adept at making technical matters quite understandable. Once he took me on a fascinating tour of a number of churches and even a cathedral just so I could see firsthand some of his favorite settings. Great pipe-organs were number one for him. He said he would, if forced, condescend to using other models, but it was obvious he considered this beneath his dignity.

"Karen," I said to my wife, "you've just got to get to know Harry better. This is an amazing person who's started attending our church."

So she fixed dinner, and together we enjoyed an evening listening to his seemingly endless anecdotes, many about prominent people he knew high up in the musical world. Harry also talked occasionally about preachers he had to endure listening to until he could finally conclude a service or convention with a final glorious flourish on his instrument.

"Did I tell you about the time So-and-so was speaking and he went on so long I finally just started playing the introduction to a closing hymn? Oh, he was furious with me, but I wouldn't back down, and the crowd cheered for me."

"You're kidding!"

"No, I'm serious. You can ask anyone who was there. It was at the University Auditorium in Valparaiso, at the denominational conference of…"

That was the first time I recall suspecting Harry might occasionally exaggerate the facts. Then it happened again. On this occasion, the details were slightly different from the first time he related this story. Little by little, doubts started creeping into my mind. But never did they come anywhere near the truth I would soon discover.

One night we were together at a small church meeting, and some of the folk wanted to sing. Harry was asked to play the piano. "No, no," he protested. "You know my instrument is the organ. You have to realize you're coming close to insulting me."

"Come on. Just tonight." But Harry dug in his heels. *That's funny*, I thought. *All these months I've known Harry, I don't think I've ever actually heard him play anything.*

Out of curiosity, I called a large church on the north side of the city where he said he'd been on staff for several years. "Hello, I'm calling about a former organist of yours named Harry Marvel. I was wondering if I could get a recommendation regarding his skills. … You say you know him, but he never worked there as an organist, just attended services for a while? I see. … What's that, you didn't know he played the organ?"

The next time I met with Harry, I asked the name of the person he had studied under. Not suspecting anything, I'm sure, he said he was, in fact, taking special advanced training at the moment from a certain exceptional organ-professor at a nearby college.

I kept the name in my mind and later made a call. It turned out this "professor" didn't work at the school but had recently been a grad student there. I managed to get the phone number of where he taught privately. So now it was back to the phone.

"Do you have someone by the name of Harry Marvel as a student? Good … Well, sir, I'm a minister, and we're thinking of having him give a recital for our congregation. Could you give me an evaluation of his skills?"

There was kind of a chuckle at the other end of the line, and then the gentleman said, "I suppose you know, so far he's only had maybe eight or ten lessons."

"With you?" I asked.

"In his life," was the reply. "I'm sure I'm his first teacher. He's a beginner student. He's just starting to get the knack of reading notes."

"You're talking about Harry Marvel, a man about 26, maybe 30 at the most?"

"Yes, Harry Marvel, why?"

"Well, I'm surprised, I guess. But thank you so much for your time and this information." "Surprised"—I was *shocked!*

Because I truly cared for Harry as a person, I arranged to meet him at a restaurant in Chicago's Loop. There I reviewed for him what I'd learned. "Oh, no," he replied, "you must have called the wrong teacher." But he couldn't fool me anymore.

"Let me help you, Harry," I said as graciously as possible. "I think we can lick this together."

"No, no!" he protested. "You don't believe me! I can tell. I thought we were close friends. How could you do something like this!" Then he got up and left without even saying goodbye. Within a few weeks, I learned he had moved to the East Coast, where I suppose the same routine was begun afresh with someone else. It's an amazing story, and the pity is, I think Harry playacted the organ-virtuoso role so long he actually believed it.

It's been years since I last thought about Harry Marvel, but he came to mind as I struggled to come up with a way of describing another problem that remains prevalent. It's the big criticism outsiders level against us: "You Christians talk a better game than you live." Restated, the average believer knows more about what the Bible teaches than they put into practice. In spite of all the preaching heard week after week throughout this land, most church members still have trouble being all that Christ-like. When it's time for the music of the church to capture outsiders with its beauty, in all too many cases we "musicians" are still learning to play our instruments.

Whereas pastors want their people's lives to reflect the principles they hear from the pulpit, their sermons don't often help that much with specific how-tos. When I conduct preaching seminars with groups of ministers and we get to work with a given passage of Scripture, this is where their sermon skills most often come up short. They struggle knowing how to move their listeners from point A to point B.

I say to them something like this: "In our chosen text, Philippians 4:8, Paul writes that you are to *fix your thoughts on what is true and honorable and right. Think about things that are pure and lovely and admirable. Think about things that are excellent and worthy of praise!*' Now, is this where your people are? When they watch TV, read a book or magazine, surf the Web, will this verse be something that guides their behavior? Why or why not? When they talk on the phone, or in the school cafeteria, over a business luncheon, during a workout at the sports center, will your sermon come to mind and be put into practice? The human mind is phenomenal. When it can wander wherever it wants because it has free time, do people train their brains to think about what's true and honorable and right and pure and lovely and admirable and excellent and worthy of praise? What will you say, as their pastor, that helps your church members and attendees to train their minds in this way? If you don't know what to tell them, believe me, they probably won't be able to figure it out on their own. Listen closely: This is the hardest work of your sermon preparation."

If Harry Marvel had stuck around instead of running off, I would have been very challenged to design ways to help him. Working with a pathology like this demands untold exertions from those of us in ministry. I do know, with God's involvement, I'd have given it my best shot. Those are also my feelings as I wrestle with the problems presented in this book; I feel as though I am in the death grip, a calling that won't let me go and that I can't abandon—sermons being swallowed up every Sunday in churches around the country, sinking into that abyss, the "Black Hole," before God's Word can transform lives. This is the battle I believe I am being called to fight—with your help.

It took years to devise the 4 simple questions I felt had wide-ranging application. They needed to be accessible for the less-than-exceptional preacher, and challenging for those with greater potential. Over many conference seasons I tested them on hundreds of ministers to see if they felt they were fair, and if they really helped when used.

Then the questions had to be understandable for laypeople, a sermon-evaluation methodology they could use that was not too complicated—or they just wouldn't use it. The questions needed to be usable for those without any speech theory, as they began to function as teachers and communicators themselves. These questions had to be a good survey tool, one that would give a pastor a handle on how well his or her people were hearing what was preached, then how readily they were adapting the truths of each sermon to everyday living, to the Mondays, Tuesdays, Wednesdays, Thursdays, Fridays and Saturdays beyond Sunday.

In all honesty, I seldom had any pastor or priest be anything but affirmative. That's probably because none of them had yet experienced the frustration of a parishioner saying, "I understand that the topic of your sermon was how we are to think Christianly. I also know what the various words mean like *true, honorable, pure,* and the others. You did a good job with those. The problem is that I don't know how to think this new way. Much of what I carry in my mind is not all that pure or honorable. I'm just being honest with you, Reverend. But that's how I've lived for about as long as I remember. I'm admitting to you that I don't know how to get to what you're describing. I may have missed it, but I don't think your sermon provided me with that kind of help."

This is when preachers begin to suspect that the four seemingly simple sermon-evaluation questions are going to cause a shift of seismic proportions in their approach.

At such a time I suppose speakers should be honored that listeners like this paid such close attention. But after any number of similar encounters during the course of a given month, ministers might wish their people had never heard of the four simple questions every sermon should answer, and especially not question three about how-tos!

My desire is to bring about positive change in the way preaching is done. But I am keenly aware that by helping the pew, I could unwittingly be destroying some pastors. I pray that doesn't happen, and I would view such a result as most unfortunate.

I hope my 4 simple questions will lead to fewer criticisms about less-important matters, like "Why are women quoted in your sermons less frequently than men?", "Why did you stoop to using a movie clip in your message?" or "Can't we get more Old Testament-based sermons from you?" But when a preacher hears repeatedly that the how-to question isn't being addressed satisfactorily, and that's already an area most ministers admit is a weakness, the comments can be extremely annoying.

Hey, I warned you that resolving the Sermon-Sucking Black Hole problem is not going to be easy. I assure you there will be many times when individuals who wear the collar and those who don't will both feel like saying, "I don't need this! I'm out of here!"

Living a lie isn't the answer either. Can you think of anything more pathetic than my friend Harry Marvel, who dreamed of being a great organist and constructed, in his mid-20s, a whole fantasy about his musical proficiency? What a divide must exist in the minds of those who choose to fabricate an environment structured from total untruth! Yet the church also is participating in a Harry Marvel syndrome, and it must face this serious problem that's been in the making for many years. We're living a lie if we pretend that all the effort, all the labor, all the work to prepare sermons that are preached from thousands of pulpits all over the land, are helping to transform lives of millions of people. This fantasy will not be resolved quickly. Listen to me carefully, however: There is hope for a solution, as long as none of us insist the church is already all that Christ-like. If we are willing to face the hard reality that we actually do not know how to play magnificent music—if we stop pretending that the real problem is not with us, but with the other guys—*then* we have an opportunity to work together, clergy and laypeople, to create a truth that will impact us beyond anything we've dreamed possible.

Indeed the truth does set us free. We need to say, "This is no longer working." Only then can we ask, "What exciting things can we do that will make a difference?"

One Last Thought

Give me a random group of ministers to work with, and I can pretty accurately predict their responses to what I'll present. Most of them will say that some, but not very many, in their congregation, are living in a way that would meet Jesus' expectations were He to assume the pastoral role. They would also admit they're not sure how to solve this problem. That's in spite of the fact most of them feel they are living the Christ-life at a level above that of their people.

Of course ministers have the decided advantage of not having to spend 40 hours a week or more at a secular job. On top of that, every seven days they are responsible to prepare and deliver a sermon about being Christ-like, and that tends to keep them spiritually focused.

Most in the group would also respond positively to the four points I say every sermon should cover. They like the questions; it's coming up with the answers that's the hard part. Especially they will have difficulty with number three—providing their people with practical "how-tos."

I personally am convinced this problem will not be solved until ministers and their people start talking together about sermons BEFORE THEY ARE PREACHED. Agreeing on a good subject and the response being called for will be the easy part. Coming up with the steps necessary to get to where all of us should be spiritually will prove the harder task. But if we can just start working together, I believe we can do it!

Chapter 10

The Sermon as Part of a Whole

....

Watching Shakespeare plays has been a diversion my wife and I have enjoyed all our married lives. We have seen well over 175 different productions.

"I didn't know the Bard wrote that many plays," a friend commented.

"He didn't," I answered. "We've seen some of his more popular titles any number of times."

My personal favorite is *King Lear*. When not performed well, it's also the play I like the least. It's about a monarch who waits too long to pass on his power. When he finally gets around to it, his mind isn't as keen as it once was, and he makes some unfortunate decisions. Actually, they're tragic mistakes.

If you've known someone with Alzheimer's, you have a feel for how I believe *King Lear* is best interpreted. I've seen him played as nothing more than an aging, raging tyrant. Most of the lines are hollered, and there's little redeeming value to the character. At the play's end the crowd claps politely, mainly because the yelling has finally stopped.

When the character is presented as an aged monarch suffering from progressive stages of dementia, the spoken lines come out as confused, with some thoughts that are almost whispered by the struggling ruler, then there is great empathy for the befuddled, pitiful old man, and an audience that is profoundly moved is on its feet, applauding because theatre has once again been magical.

Chicago, the part of the country I call home, has a new multimillion-dollar Shakespeare theatre beside Lake Michigan out on Navy Pier. The company has been very successful, and tickets aren't easy to get. Recently it staged *Lear* with a fairly young actor playing the aging king. I had misgivings about him maybe being a screamer, but just the opposite proved true. He handled the part beautifully. The director's touch was sensitive, and the staging, costumes, sound, and lighting were all excellent as well.

The most famous scene comes near the end of the story. As the disturbed king walks with his fool on a stormy night, you can almost see the old man descend into madness. As the thunder cracks, so does his mind. Lightning is standard in this sequence. But in the Chicago production, it also rained on the actors—not just a sprinkle, but a real tempest. The audience stayed dry, but the two men on stage were getting drenched.

Our Saturday tickets were for the 4 p.m. performance so we could go to dinner afterwards in Greektown and still be home and in bed before ten, then get up early and be ready for 9:30 church the next morning. But the contrast between the events of Saturday late afternoon and Sunday morning was so great, it took my breath away.

It's not that I expect church to compete with theatre. In many ways it can't. Then again, theatre can't compete with church either; particularly when church is about the business of healing and redemption, it is unsurpassable. What hit me so hard when I thought about it, was that the Saturday production had been a collaborative effort with 60 or 70 people all working together in a most incredible way, each doing his or her individual job at peak efficiency to pull off a stellar performance.

The number involved in the Sunday service was sizeable as well, if you include ushers, children's workers, musicians in the choir and worship teams, etc. But too many churches approach the church service like stringing unmatched beads on a wire, unrelated elements with no connection that the average person would comprehend. I really tried to find some sort of linkage that Sunday morning, but it escaped me. In truth, there probably *was* none. I say that because for too long, the contributors in the average church service have been people doing their own shtick, with little effort to make the parts mesh. The worship music is a package unto itself; the minister preaches on a totally different topic; the prayer, the Scripture readings, the closing benediction—none of them fit into a whole.

Why is this?

I'm convinced the main reason is that ministers aren't able to say far enough in advance, "This is my subject. Here's the response I'm calling for." The how-to and the how-long don't have to be determined as far in advance; just answering the first two simple questions is plenty sufficient. But coming up with the answers the day before is too late. If at all possible, these matters need to be addressed a couple weeks in advance. Otherwise, how can someone write a drama script and get people to memorize their lines and rehearse together? Can a parish musician find fitting music and have time to practice when everything is last-minute? I love when Scripture readers memorize the passage and say it with great feeling, but again, it takes advanced planning. When surveyed about their response to parts of the worship service, laypeople listed the Scripture reading as the "most boring" part. There are countless ways to present it in a creative, attention-getting manner, but if people don't have time to brainstorm, script and prepare these weekly passages, the readings will have a ho-hum familiarity.

The four simple sermon-evaluation questions are designed to allow for a bridge between the sermon material and the worship teams so our services are shot throughout with contemporary meaning. The use of these questions in the right way ensures not only unforgettable sermons, but unforgettable Sunday worship services.

Building a service around a given theme isn't hard once the person preaching can state early on what the sermon's subject and response will be. It's not enough to say, "I'll preach on Psalm 1." A soloist could go home, read the psalm's six verses, and decide to sing a song about a tree! "After all, doesn't verse 3 read, *'He is like a tree planted by streams of water, which yields its fruit in season and whose leaf does not wither'?"*

How much better to say, "My subject is *Knowing God's Blessing in Your Life*, and the response I'm going for is to have people consistently get their counsel from the right source, not from the wrong ones." Further input to worship-planners could be given about what the intended sources might be, but a clear direction can be established in just a sentence or two by providing the subject and response. At this point, planning a coordinated service shouldn't be too difficult, and I believe many volunteers from the congregation would be delighted to help. Here we begin to enter into true partnership—not just preachers and listeners creating co-meaning during the sermon event, but a vast conspiracy on behalf of pulpit and pew, finding ways to make the sermon the jewel of a harmonious, unified whole during the Sunday service.

For example, for what shall we then praise God? Remember, we have been working with the Psalm 1 passage through most of this book. "Worship" means to attribute worth to God, so which attribute(s) should be emphasized during that part of the service? Any number of choices would be appropriate. For example...

- God is wise. He knows what is best for us.
- God is life. Who better understands how we tick?
- God is a wonderful counselor who gives us great advice.
- God is Truth, and He shares His thoughts with us.
- God is good. He wants to provide us with the finest there is.

More suggestions could be made, but you get the idea. Obviously, the worship and preaching themes should connect. If every song or Scripture in the service doesn't fit into a cohesive whole, at least some of them should!

The worship direction should probably *not* be one of the following:

- God is jealous. (He is, but how does that relate to the given preaching theme of *Knowing God's Blessings in Your Life*?)
- God is Creator, and yes, the maker of trees! (But save that solo for another time!)
- God is omnipotent. (But why explore that theme when it's not appropriate for the given sermon?)
- God is holy. (This might fit if you force it. But it's not the best choice.)
- God is Spirit, and God is love, etc., etc. (From the long list of divine characteristics, pick the ones most appropriate to the sermon subject, but believe me, it won't be one of these two.)

Once a related worship theme is chosen, all kinds of creative possibilities occur. Perhaps a given Sunday you want someone in the congregation, other than the minister, to offer the morning prayer.

- Father in heaven, as a high-school counselor, I do my best to offer good advice to students who come to me for help. It's not always easy, and not everyone heeds my words. But because of my experience I was asked to speak to You in praise for being a wonderful counselor...

- Dear Heavenly Father, I'm not used to getting up in front of people in this condition. As you know I'm now almost eight months pregnant. I guess you could say I'm full of life, but then, that's what we're praising You for this morning...

- Jesus, how good it is to talk to You. As a criminal investigator I'm always looking for the truth. How satisfying to finally talk to someone I never have to question. When You say something, it's the whole truth and nothing but the truth...

- God, I'm not very old. Last week I had my tenth birthday. So I'm not too wise either. But I want to tell You for everyone in this church that we think You are very wise...

Having conducted hundreds of workshops, I know from experience it's fairly easy for a small group of volunteers to quickly come up with many ideas like this. It's not so much a creativity issue as it is being able to connect with a specific subject and response, plus an appropriate worship theme. When that's done, laypeople can be trained to ask simple questions about the service elements such as, "Who might be a good person in the congregation we could ask to say the morning prayer?"

Additional questions would sound like, "Can anyone think of a song that captures what the pastor is saying about getting our counsel from wise sources?" "What Scriptures are there that emphasize this same truth and could be read right before the sermon?" "How about a volunteer to find a quote or two about places to go for good counsel?" Some kind of contemporary source would be good; we often turn to the tried-and-true and overly familiar. Many of these resources could even be projected on a screen during the prelude or the offering.

What keeps simple connections like these from being made week after week by people other than the pastor is the lack of a clear direction established early on regarding the thrust of the sermon. That's because most ministers' preparation involves them in all kinds of homework that doesn't quickly get them to the nub of what they plan to preach.

I realize the thrust of this chapter seems to focus on responsibility that falls mainly within the pastor's domain, but if most laypeople knew how overworked (and underpaid) the average minister is, and how welcome additional help would be to lift the unrelenting task of sermon- and service-planning (even in liturgical churches where so much of the service appears to be formatted), parishioners wouldn't hesitate to volunteer to lift the load of 52 Sundays a year for understaffed clergy. Ministers wrestle with how well what they do in the pulpit and on the platform meets the people in the pew through significant weekly encounters. Your offer, "Can I help in any way in service-planning?" might be just the answer to their prayers. This chapter gives you an idea how to proceed.

One of the reasons for the huge Sermon-Sucking Black Hole in churches is that by the time for the sermon, people's minds have already been pulled in too many different directions. *King Lear*, written by a literary master, is one well-crafted storyline from beginning to end, and experiencing the play can be extremely satisfying. It wouldn't be if the director decided to insert a speech from *Hamlet* here or some comic relief from *The Merry Wives of Windsor* there. This same kind of unintended dissonance is created when even good parts of a church service fight each other, when a well-crafted theme isn't followed from start to finish.

Am I making too much of something that's really not that important? If during the week people quickly recalled what Scriptures were read in church, what music was sung, what prayers were said or sermons preached, I'd back off. But that's not the case. So excuse me if it seems like I'm raining on something you're reluctant to criticize. I'm calling for strategic changes before an impending storm blows down the house.

One Last Thought

A unique cross, popular today among Presbyterians, was used by the monastic community founded by St. Columba at Iona. It's a Latin cross with a ring around the intersection of the two arms, which is called a Celtic cross.

An expression of praise often found in the psalms is still used today by many believers. Though most Christians can't define precisely what it means, when they say or sing "hallelujah" they believe they are worshiping the Lord.

The church calendar begins with the Season of Advent. "Advent" means "coming" and refers to both the First and Second Advents of Jesus.

Present-day Israel and Jordan make up most of the ancient land of Canaan, where the majority of the events of the Bible took place.

Oliver Cromwell (1599–1658) was the leader of the forces of Parliament and Protestantism against Charles I of England. The "Ironsides," his psalm-singing regiments, were never defeated.

And did I have in mind a way these religion-related paragraphs fit together? Not really! I was just attempting to illustrate what all too many church services are like. They certainly sound spiritual, but they go in a dozen different directions. Little wonder that after a while, lots of people stop paying attention to what's happening.

Check yours out to see if it is characterized this way. If not ... well, "hallelujah"!

Chapter 11

Rat-a-tat-tat:
The Power of Repetition

··

Over 30 years ago, an older acquaintance told me about an incident in his life that I've never forgotten. Having enlisted in the Navy during the Second World War, he was eventually put on a ship leaving the west coast, bound for the Philippines. Also on board was the world's flyweight boxing champion, who was returning to his homeland after having successfully defended his title in the States.

His story was as follows:

"To stay in shape the little boxer trained on board ship. We watched and then one day he offered to go three rounds with anyone willing to take him on. With not much else to do I decided right on the spot to try it. I'm a big man and he was so small I didn't figure he could hurt me all that much. Having boxed a little in college, it would be fun to see if I could land my right-hand haymaker.

"Round one in the sun was me chasing him and swinging mainly with my power right, but he was too quick for me. I never actually connected. All this peewee guy did was dance around and rat-a-tat-tat me repeatedly. Rat-a-tat-tat. Rat-a-tat-tat. Rat-a-tat-tat. Rat-a-tat-tat. He was like an obnoxious fly you want to swat, but right when you go to smack him—he's not there anymore. My buddies cheered me on and before I knew it the first round was over. A bit winded, if anything I was more confident now—I figured his rat-a-tat-tats didn't hurt much. So in round two I'd ignore them and just go after him with every bit of firepower I had.

"Before everything was totally sorted out in my head the bell sounded and I jumped up, determined to corner this guy and pound him like he deserved for being so cocky. But unfortunately, it was almost like round one all over again. It was rat-a-tat-tat, rat-a-tat-tat on my arms and stomach, with me swinging big round houses but not being able to really land a solid shot. He was just incredibly fast and clever. Rat-a-tat-tat. Like a miniature machine he would nail me four, five, six quick punches in a row and then vanish. In and out he worked. Rat-a-tat-tat. Now when I punched and missed I could hear my buddies laughing. Some of them actually started cheering for the foreign champ. Toward the end of the round I remember thanking God there were only three minutes left to go and I hoped I could make it because those rat-a-tat-tats were starting to get to me!

"The last round proved to be pure torture from beginning to end. I was exhausted and knew I had met my match. Rat-a-tat-tat and more rat-a-tat-tats. My arms and body were so sore from those *[expletive deleted]* rat-a-tat-tats. I tried my best to smack his face because I could tell by his big grin he was having great fun at my expense. But I couldn't get near. My blows were less frequent now. They were also slower and easier to dodge. I knew there wasn't going to be a big knockout on my part. Unfortunately, he knew that too. Rat-a-tat-tat. *If he rat-a-tat-tats me one more time I think I'll die right here on the ship's deck.* Rat-a-tat-tat. *Oh no, he did it!* Rat-a-tat-tat. *The little devil just did it again.* Rat-a-tat-tat. *And again. God help me please, no more rat-a-tat-tats,* I prayed. Then as if the Almighty heard my plea the bell kindly sounded and put an end to my misery!"

When it comes to communication theory, I'm a strong advocate of the rat-a-tat-tat school of thought. It seems that we humans need a cumulative total of "punches" for the Holy Spirit to get our attention. Pastors in the pulpit and laypeople at their teaching podiums need to make sure the message is relevant, simple and clear. Zero in on the subject, response, how-to, and how-long. Then in as many elements of the worship service as possible, the basic concept is repeated for people again and again. And again and again. Rat-a-tat-tat. Rat-a-tat-tat. Rat-a-tat-tat!

Long ago the advertising world discovered this method. Reduce what you want to say to its essence. Put it into a 30-second spot, or a 60-second one if you have more money to spend. Then play it over and over hundreds and hundreds of times. Rat-a-tat-tat. Rat-a-tat-tat. Madison Avenue understands that a consumer doesn't even know a product exists until he or she has heard about it at least 18 times. It's the repetition that starts getting to people. Eventually they finally do try one of Arby's new Market Fresh Sandwiches, or test-drive an Accord, or decide to "fly the friendly skies" of United.

With a captive audience for a whole hour or more each Sunday morning, are there reasons the church hasn't explored this technique? Probably so. To start with, Kingdom living can't be reduced to a catchphrase like "Please don't squeeze the Charmin." Nevertheless, just ensuring that each week the four simple sermon questions—*Subject? Response? How to? How long?*—are clearly answered will quickly improve matters.

Another consideration as to why the repetitive approach is not being used is that ministers are busy people. Their days are seldom predictable. I've often said that if a pastor ever had a miracle week with no appointments other than normal meetings, the hours would still fill up and require more time than any layperson can imagine. There's always an unexpected funeral, a crisis counseling situation, or an emergency with one of the missionaries the church supports. Being in the pastorate means being on-call 24/7; it is a profession where it's almost impossible to get ahead of the schedule.

Another factor stems from ministers' busy schedules: Because they already have too many meetings, few have learned the joy of getting their people involved in the routine of brainstorming sermons or the key role of helping with service-planning. Once a pastor introduces a regular format of lay involvement and participation, it will save hours. As I've said before, I did this throughout the 10 years I was in an inner-city church plant. I brainstormed the services with members of the congregation weekly, and I sat down with listeners a half-hour after preaching on Sunday to get questions, comments and feedback about the morning's preaching. I discovered I not only had created a team of brainstormers, but my laypeople became researchers, media consultants, creative advisors, hands-on go-to folk, and errand-runners all working to pull together meaningful worship services every Sunday.

As for the how the service is laid out, here is where the rat-a-tat-tat factor can be most effective. Yes, the theme should be preached well. That's a given. But given the chance to contribute, feeling their ideas and opinions are respected, laypeople will go to great lengths to discover music about the topic or some related worship theme. They'll tie the direction of the sermon into the prayer; read related Scriptures about it; line up testimonies that underscore the same truth; put up visual reminders like banners and posters; create and project the concept; write, dramatize and act out scripts. They will design how-tos, formulate practical assignments so people don't forget during the week this important word from the Lord. Rat-a-tat-tat. Take *that*, Sermon-Sucking Black Hole!

You, the layperson, are absolutely essential to this process, and you can save your overworked pastor a ton of effort.

Busy pastors know about delegating. How else would the many tasks of the church get done—the youth ministry, the business matters, the janitorial work, the visitor follow-up, the missions program, the communion preparation, the retreats, the children's programs, the correspondence? Delegation is practically the name of the game. For some reason, assigning worship-service responsibilities to worthy, eager laypeople is almost an unknown. Maybe this is still a bit too protected an area for most pastors to let go of.

Granted, lots of churches have hired music ministers, and their activity is a big part of the Sunday morning experience. (How many times the music and message are actually synchronized is another matter.) This traditional staff position does set a precedent, though; if the minister can assign to the hired musician the worship-music responsibility, can't successful ways be found to delegate other worship tasks to key laypeople? I can't imagine many settings where the preaching pastor would want the responsibility again of being in charge of the music once a skilled professional has been put in place to bear the load of research, contact work, rehearsals, accompaniment, etc.

Hiring additional staff for areas like drama is usually not feasible except in large congregations, so the solution still rests with volunteers taking on such assignments. I believe many would be eager to do so if given the opportunity. Unfortunately, people skilled in these areas usually don't know how to go about offering their help. That is a problem that still needs to be addressed.

First, I'll throw in a caution. A system needs to be in place that allows volunteers several weeks' lead time to work on elements like creative Scripture readings, banners, special prayers, calls to worship, posters, dramas, etc. Last-minute assignments quickly burn people out; volunteers have demanding jobs as well and can only rally to enormous effort so many times. Also, these elements should all correlate with the direction of the sermon, or the efforts are actually counterproductive. Doing your own thing with little understanding of where the rest of the service is going really isn't satisfying.

On the other hand, when all the pieces fit together on a given Sunday, no job is thought too hard, no effort too great, no challenge too difficult. People will knock themselves out time and again if what they do is meaningful and integral to the work of the Lord. The Holy Spirit, during our pre-planning brainstorm sessions, often put into our hearts something we had no idea would have the impact that it did during the service. A prayer from someone who lost a child was planned, without human foreknowledge, to be prayed on the very week that another family's son was killed in a boating accident. Think what kind of empowering goes on for the worship-planning team when these divinely coordinated incidents occur. People become convinced that they are working in league with a human team, but more than that, in collegiality with the divine.

It's incredibly satisfying to participate in a service where the worship theme is a perfect prelude for what follows, where the prayer clearly ties into the overall direction of the morning. Later, the drama sets up the sermon beautifully, and the music that follows fits hand in glove with what the message is about. The testimony makes the truth personal and alive, and the creative Scripture reading is like God Himself putting His stamp of approval on everything. Little wonder so many respond to the closing challenge when it's given. Repetition has reinforced the basic concept again and again. All this planning needs to be thought as an act of compassion; we're not doing creative service-planning for the sake of being clever or of showing off. We seek to design a whole service for the sake of those people whose minds and hearts are hungry for spiritual meaning. We work hard together, pastor and laypeople, for the sake of the rest of the congregation.

Preachers who think "one big blow is the way to go" and little else is needed, can go ahead and content themselves with rare moments of success. But treating sermons as the main event and everything else in the service as "preliminaries" is no longer where transforming churches are. And if those haymaker sermons keep missing the mark for some reason, and the pastor knows they are less than exceptional, the ministry can become a tiring and frustrating calling!

In most settings, it's been so long since everything connected in a church service that many of my readers have little firsthand knowledge how powerful such an experience can be. The pity is, it doesn't take all that much effort to make it work. There are two keys. First is knowing the sermon subject and response. Second is having this information at least several weeks ahead of time.

One point about the second key: If a preacher had to have the whole sermon outlined for lay teams to begin planning, it would detonate my whole worship-service concept. Again, we're going for simple solutions. All he or she has to do is determine the subject and response (then stick to it—no changing ideas midstream). This is a huge freedom for preachers, and it gives powerful direction for the planners. It also gives the speakers direction they can cling to when unforeseen crises sabotage an already-busy week. *What was I going to preach on? Oh, yes. Here's my subject and desired response.*

Let me also remind you that the Holy Spirit, not being time-bound, is perfectly capable of leading in preaching directions and worship-planning two, three, or five weeks ahead, just as He is in giving direction for tomorrow or for this coming Sunday. It's ridiculous of us to limit Him with our finite understandings of inspiration.

Here's a how-to for those interested in volunteering your service-planning helps. I'd suggest you target a special Sunday in the future. Some options could be Super Bowl Sunday, Martin Luther King, Jr. Sunday, National Day of Prayer Sunday, Mother's Day, Father's Day, Independence Day Sunday or Thanksgiving Sunday. Avoid major holidays like Christmas and Easter; the church will likely have special plans already in place.

Talk with a couple friends who might share your interest and form a small group. Settle on a Sunday you're all interested in working on, and set up an appointment with your minister. What you want to talk about is volunteering, *under the pastor's guidance,* to help plan the morning service for that given date. You are not going to create a Wild West rodeo of innovative events. Your desire is to help the pastor, lift the load, and make lay feedback and participation possible.

First, for your own sake, review the suggestions in Ch. 6. Have you been praying for your pastor consistently? Loving your pastor as Jesus does? Taking notes during your pastor's sermons? Complimenting your pastor whenever possible? If you are doing these things, you are now ready to offer your help if your pastor seems open to the idea.

Let me repeat, because this is important: Your input is not to be presented as a huge makeover of the entire service. What you have to offer might be nothing more than a suggestion regarding the music, or working on a banner. Offer your help, stress that this is only if your pastor feels comfortable working with your small lay team, and state that you want to be respectful of the parameters of worship-planning and expression that are in conformity to his/her style. Be careful to work within your minister's comfort zone.

One last caution: The last thing you ever want to do is rat-a-tat-tat your minister. He or she gets enough of that already. Your job is to cheer your pastor on and to be a helper if your minister is comfortable with your offer.

One Last Thought
When leading lay workshops on Planning Creative Church Services, I like to suggest thinking about a Sunday service as having three parts:

1. *The Approach to God in Worship*
2. *God Speaking Through His Written Word*
3. *The Response of Obedience*

I'm not sure where I first picked up on this format. But people new to the process of service-planning, and somewhat intimidated by it, seem to find these divisions helpful. What they do is to divide a service into understandable parts and provide a way for the diverse thinking in a group to quickly be brought together.

The Approach to God in Worship is basically a time to focus on a specific aspect of who God is and why praising Him for this given attribute is appropriate.

God Speaking Through His Written Word is a different dynamic. Central to this section is the sermon, but it can also include reading related Scriptures, special music that sets up or repeats the theme of the message, drama, etc.

During *The Response of Obedience* people express their reaction to what they have heard from the Lord. This can be done through prayer, music, a responsive reading, invitations, the Lord's Table, and numerous other examples.

My experience has been that participants find this suggested format helpful, and have little trouble adopting to their own situation what they have learned.

Chapter 12

Practice Planning: Mother's Day

....

L et's practice planning a service. Mother's Day, the second Sunday of May—let's say that's the date you target.

It's not a bad choice. If your pastor has been at the church for years, there's a good chance most of the creative Mother's Day ideas were used up some time back.

So you phone and ask for a half-hour appointment. The reason you give is that you'd like to see if there might be a way you can help work on the Mother's Day service this year. What you have in mind is suggesting maybe one or two elements you can help with. First, you want to know the direction the sermon is going. Even being given the biblical text that's been chosen would be great.

I'll be the token pastor, okay? So you begin that first meeting something like this.

You: I appreciate the chance to see you, Dr. Mains. I feel a little presumptuous offering to help plan a service. But then you do your job so well, I thought even if I'm out of place asking to do this, Dr. Mains will still be gracious and kind.

Dr. Mains: Well, I would hope so. Tell me what kind of ideas you have in mind.

You: It could be as simple as a Mother's Day poem someone memorizes, or a special Scripture reading with several voices. Then again, I'm game for putting together a series of candid photos of mothers in the church that could be projected during a solo or reading. Since it's almost two months away, I was hoping something really nice could be done. I'm certainly open to suggestions you have. But first I thought it was best to get an idea of what you might be preaching on.

Dr. Mains: When my secretary told me what you had in mind, I actually started looking for a text. I do have one I'm leaning toward. I like it because everyone in the church ought to be able to relate to it. I think too many times I've preached exclusively to mothers on Mother's Day. This is Proverbs 23:25. Here's how it reads in the New Living Translation: *"So give your parents joy! May she who gave you birth be happy."* I could direct that sermon to everyone. "The one who gave you birth, or the person who filled the mother role for you—do your best to make her happy." That way the men shouldn't nod off.

You: Or listen to see if their wife measures up to the qualities of the virtuous woman in Proverbs 31.

Dr. Mains: Right … actually, I've been writing down some ideas about how to make our mothers happy. Think I can even give a suggestion to those whose mothers have died, which is my situation.

You: Then your subject would be the mothers of everyone present in the service. In my case, my mother.

Dr. Mains: I guess you could say that.

You: I was trying to picture all of those women in my mind. And you're going to encourage each of us to make our mother happy. What if the relationship with somebody's mom isn't good?

Dr. Mains: Actually, that's what got me thinking about this text. I read an article about a mother who was murdered and her daughter didn't find out about it for several months because they weren't on speaking terms.

You: Oh my!

Dr. Mains: Sad, isn't it?

You: Certainly is. I wonder, could I make a suggestion?

Dr. Mains: Sure.

You: Don't change anything. This sounds like a great text and a most interesting topic with a clear response—"make your mother happy." You just have to tell us how to do that. I'll be interested to hear what you have to say. And with this information, here's what I'm thinking: I'd like a week to consider what I might like to work on related to the service. Could I call you in a week with a specific idea or two?

Dr. Mains: *(ending the conversation)* That'd be fine. I'll wait to hear from you.

Wouldn't it be great if every meeting was as quick and smooth as I imagined? It's quite possible your pastor will not be used to working on sermons a month or two in advance. Then again, some initial thoughts about the direction of the message could be forming. Possibly the time is best spent trying to clarify the basic sermon idea. Some ministers will find this beneficial; others might see it as threatening. But don't offer to start working on your part until the subject and response of the sermon are nailed down.

Having these two pieces in place frees you and your friends to begin thinking about one or two service elements that can enhance that morning. Do a good job with this assignment, and it should open the door for greater involvement in the future.

You now have a week to consider what you want to suggest. A good question to begin with is what worship theme would complement the direction of this message about mothers of those in the church and how to make them happy. A praise focus on the love of God that overcomes all barriers might make sense.

Begin looking through scripture for verses about God's great love for us. A passage like Isaiah 49:14–16 could prove helpful because it uses mother imagery:

> But Zion said, "The LORD has forsaken me, the Lord has forgotten me." "Can a mother forget the baby at her breast and have no compassion on the child she has borne? Though she may forget, I will not forget you! See, I have engraved you on the palms of my hands; your walls are ever before me."

God's unfailing love is also a major theme in many of the psalms and certainly in numerous hymns.

That thought about picturing all the mothers of the church keeps coming back to you. How unique each mother is and how special. Wouldn't it be great if a picture of each one could be hung in a gallery for every person in attendance to see? That's probably too daunting a task to execute. What about a projection of as many mothers' faces as possible, while a poem about mothers is read or a song sung? Having enough time to work on a project like this makes it manageable. How would an announcement in the church bulletin read?

This Mother's Day, Pastor Mains will be preaching about Mom and how to make her happy. Kids, adults—find a photo you like of your mother. Put it in an envelope with your name, address and phone and leave it at the church office by the end of April. It will be returned to you. During the Mother's Day service, we want to project pictures of as many moms as possible to honor them. You'll be disappointed if your mother is missing!

Don't worry about polishing the words yet. It's still just a working idea. You only put the thoughts on paper so the concept can be easily communicated.

There must be a zillion poems written about mothers. Check the local library for resources they have. Look for one that talks about each mother being unique. Also appropriate quotes—especially if they relate to making a mother happy.

As Mother's Day gets closer, what will marketers suggest as the way to bring your mother delight? Check last year's newspapers and magazines for advertisements. Write down easily recognizable catchphrases.

Are there short readings or brief dramas on the topic you can locate?

What about someone in attendance that morning who only has negative thoughts about a mother? Could there be some present who, like the daughter in the article mentioned, aren't on speaking terms with their mothers? What might relate to them?

A List of Good Qualities

Maybe a list of 20–25 good qualities could be projected or listed in the church bulletin. For example, sense of humor, good cook, musical skills, praying mom, etc. Check any on the list that characterize your mother. No matter who the person is, at least a few positive attributes should be discernible.

Tell Us Something Good About Mom

How about a question like this: "If you were called on to tell us something good about your mother in just one word, what would it be? We don't want anything negative. We're looking for something positive and need that thought reduced to just one word."

Famous Mothers

Another direction: Who are some of the famous mothers in the movies or on television? What qualities make them memorable?

Sensory Memory-Joggers

What mother memories relate to your 5 senses (taste, smell, sight, sound, touch)?

Songs About Mom

Which recording artists, Christian or secular, have recorded songs on this topic?

The Best Person Possible to Pray

Who might be an appropriate person to ask to give the morning prayer? Is there someone who has adopted handicapped kids? Could a child offer a poignant prayer about moms? Match the person in a visual way to the type of prayer that needs to be prayed. Could one whole family give sentence prayers of thanksgiving for their mother?

These are random ideas, of course. Hopefully a few will point you to something that seems interesting and challenging, to craft more fully an element that relates to the theme of the morning. More specifically, the service will focus on drawing everyone present into concentrated thoughts about their mother and how they can contribute to her happiness. The morning also needs sustaining power. People shouldn't forget what they heard immediately after they leave the sanctuary. This is one Sunday the Black Hole effect definitely needs to be reversed.

Start making notes; do whatever research is appropriate. Also, let your mind have a day or two for processing or refining some of the possibilities.

Before too long you will want to pick one, two, or three concepts that especially appeal to you. These are the ones you will pitch when you make your phone call to the pastor. What you are offering is to see to it that two of them will be ready and polished for the upcoming Mother's Day service. Quite possibly this will mean needing to enlist the help of others. But you're excited to get going on things.

With everything moving along so well, are you ready for a surprise?

One Last Thought

If you're a grandparent who wants to take your grandchildren to the Ringling Brothers Barnum & Bailey Circus you saw as a kid, you're in for a surprise. A lead article in *USA Today* informed readers that the circus isn't anything like what it was a generation or two back.

The three rings are gone and the new traveling extravaganza features "a $15 million, arena-sized blockbuster with a hip-hop musical score, a storyline to tie the acts together, a 24-foot video screen and a Latina mistress of ceremonies who was a semi-finalist on *American Idol*." The article goes on to say that these changes may be hard on old-timers, but the new generation likes what it sees.

Granted, there's a vast difference between the circus and the church, but I still believe the time has come to begin freeing God's laypeople to think more creatively about church services. Recognizing that most present-day American church services bear little resemblance to the New Testament pattern anyway, and there are already huge changes taking place, I'm anxious that creative minds in our congregations also start thinking about ways to improve how we:

1. Corporately Approach God in Worship
2. Allow Him to Speak to Us Through His Written Word
3. Respond to Him in Obedience

For Ringling Brothers it's probably a matter of adjusting or going out of business.

Come to think of it, that could be the same set of alternatives for some churches!

Chapter 13

Mother's Day Sermon:
A Working Draft

∙∙

L et's pretend your conversation proved a real incentive for me, your substitute minister, to get working immediately on the Mother's Day sermon. That's not an impossible scenario. Sermon preparation is done mostly in isolation, and interest from someone on the outside can prove highly motivating to your pastor.

So on the next Sunday I greet you with a surprise. I tell you that I actually have a working sermon manuscript and ask if you will take a few minutes to go over it before talking together on the phone.

"I'd love to," you respond, glad to have this additional input. This is the work in progress that you read…

∙∙∙∙∙∙∙∙∙∙∙∙∙∙∙∙

Mother's Day Sermon – working draft

If you've heard Dr. Laura on radio, you know she has the ability to quickly get to the heart of a matter. Day after day she demonstrates both rapid and remarkable insight into what's at the core of a caller's dilemma.

It's no wonder her program was heard on hundreds of powerful stations before she signed an exclusive long-term contract with Sirius XM Radio. Because she is socially conservative, Christian believers make up a large percentage of Dr. Laura's millions of daily listeners. That's because she holds to basic Judeo-Christian standards.

Got a problem? Call Dr. Laura. But expect her to be quite direct. She's not one to pull any punches, especially if she thinks you're partly responsible for your mess.

Then again, you can play it safe and just listen. You'll still get the impression that family problems aren't really all that complicated, if you just use common sense and hold to traditional values.

Maybe that's why the story of the death of Dr. Laura's mother came as a shock to me. First, it was disturbing that the badly decomposed body of Yolanda Schlessinger was found by the Beverly Hills, California, police. Concerned neighbors had put in a call saying they hadn't seen her for weeks. Next, the initial autopsy suggested she might have been murdered. Police said the condition of the body and of the home indicated the woman had been dead for quite a while, possibly several months.

Shortly after learning of the news, Dr. Laura issued a terse statement that addressed her mother's death and alluded to their bitter estrangement: "I am horrified by the tragic circumstances of my mother's death, and so sad to learn that she died as she chose to live— alone and isolated."

I suppose I expected that with all her insights, Dr. Laura somehow could have found a way to repair the rift. Granted, maybe it was not possible—maybe her mom was just an impossible person—but it seemed strange. And then Dr. Laura's statement—so precise and to-the-point. It felt clinical, not loving, considering it was about her mother.

Because today is Mother's Day, at the moment I don't want to spend any more time on Dr. Laura or Yolanda. Instead, let's talk about *your* mom, the woman who gave birth to you. Or the person who filled the mother role on your behalf. What's her name?

Some of the mothers you're thinking about are deceased. Others still live.

Some moms, maybe yours (apparently not Dr. Laura's) fit the saintly category. Then again, certain moms, for one reason or another, are estranged even from their own children.

Almost all mothers demonstrate good qualities. What was one of your mom's? Was she creative, businesslike, hospitable, athletic, musical? Was she a teacher, a leader?

Most of your moms also have characteristics you wish they could change. In that regard, moms are like the rest of us—some have bad tempers or bad tongues; some hold grudges, play favorites, lie; some are self-centered or self-righteous; some get hooked on drugs or even have criminal records.

But the bottom line of what I want to say this Mother's Day about *your* mother is that to the best of your ability, I want you to work at bringing her joy.

My text is Proverbs 23:25. This is how it reads in the New Living Translation: *"So give your parents joy! May she who gave you birth be happy."*

It doesn't take too much to understand what's being said, does it?

Here's the same verse in the NIV: *"May your father and mother be glad; may she who gave you birth rejoice."*

So if Dr. Laura happened to be listening today, I could be quite direct and observe that the text doesn't say, "If your mom was a wonderful person…" It simply reads, "The one who gave you birth—do your best to make her happy."

To which Dr. Laura might reply, "I said I was sad to learn that she died as she chose to live—alone and isolated."

And I would respond, "This Scripture isn't about your feelings. It just basically says to do the best you can to make your mother happy."

"I know," she might answer, "but if you knew my mother…!"

"Wait a minute, Dr. Laura," I would interrupt (as she often does with her callers). "Did you come to this service to hear my sermon, or did you want to figure out how *you're* going to rationalize away this text?"

See, I was thinking if someone's mom has already died, it's nice to drive to the grave today and leave flowers. But are there other options?

You have the opportunity to decide how you want to remember your mother. You can pass along to your kids and grandkids the precise memory you choose. None of us has a perfect mom, and none of your mom's children are all that perfect either. But God sees enough good in everyone to offer to redeem us. And can't we also look for that redeemable good, instead of only concentrating on what is ugly? Then pass that positive memory along to those who may not have known your mother as well as you did.

For example, I can say to my young granddaughter Josie, "Your middle name is Faith. That was my mother's first name. She was your great-grandmother. Here's a picture of her. Isn't she pretty? Now let me tell you something very special about her that I want you to always remember. She loved books. She loved to learn. As much as she knew, she always wanted to know more. That was one of the really good things about your great-grandmother—my mother. And I hope you'll be like she was about loving books. You actually look a little like her, don't you?"

Isn't that better than saying something negative—even if the negative is true? And I believe what I'm suggesting would make a mother happy. It would bring her joy as a parent; the one who gave you birth might even rejoice.

If your mother is alive, should you have already sent a card? Probably. But this Proverbs verse doesn't read, "May she who gave you birth be happy on Mother's Day."

That's why I put a card of my own for everyone here in each bulletin. Though it's beautifully done by artist _____, it's not for you to give to your mom. Instead, it's a *personal* reminder that hopefully you'll see often because you keep it in your Bible.

Read it aloud with me: *"So give your parents joy! May she who gave you birth be happy."* Proverbs 23:25. I had [artist's name] design this card because my words were not just meant for this Sunday, but as an ongoing reminder to give cause for *your* mother, and *your* mom, and *yours*—to rejoice!

And yes, a Mother's Day card from you might have resulted in that. In addition, I'd like to suggest a dozen other ideas if your mom is alive. Those are:

1. A short letter you write to your mother, listing qualities you really like about her (all these points to be developed more fully as I work on this sermon).
2. A phone call that brings to mind a pleasant memory.
3. A small photo album or video you put together that she will treasure.
4. A verse from Scripture that reminds you of her.
5. A poem you wrote, or found in a book, that conveys your love and respect for her.
6. A compliment someone made about her that you purposely pass along.

7. A CD of music you believe she would enjoy listening to.
8. Photos of the most handsome, beautiful and intelligent grandchildren in the world.
9. A gift of time: one hour of yours spent in whatever way she wants.
10. A cartoon or a humorous book you think will tickle her funny bone.
11. A box of candy or flowers that arrive when they're not so expected. Or…
12. Share personal prayer requests, and then take time to actually pray together—in person or over the phone—you and your mother, if that is possible.

What is God's Spirit saying to you through my words?

I ask because I may have gotten some of the specifics wrong, but I believe the Lord is saying to many here, "You certainly understand enough to make some kind of appropriate overture your mom's way. It's not really that hard to make sure the woman 'who gave you birth' experiences happiness from your hand. This is a good thing and a biblical thing to do. And you don't have to wait until next Mother's Day to put your ideas into action. Let her continually rejoice because of you—her son or daughter."

Finally, let the fate of Yolanda Schlessinger be a reminder that you don't always have forever to get things done. … And when you see this card in your Bible, allow this gift of [artist's name]'s print to motivate you to be a cause of rejoicing to that special woman who, humanly speaking, provided you with God's wonderful gift of life.

· · · · · · · · · · · · · · · ·

As you finish reading my sermon draft, I hope your mind goes to the four simple sermon questions everyone should be able to answer after hearing (or reading) a message. How does this draft sermon measure up?

What is the subject? … Mothers.

What is the desired response? … To do something that will make her happy.

What is the how-to? … While I've given 12 practical suggestions, you might have an idea or two that would be even better.

How long is this going to take? … Expect it to be an ongoing exercise because of the reminder card tucked in the Bible.

This is great, you say to yourself. *And I wonder if he has a person in mind to design the Scripture card. If not, I have an idea of someone we could ask.*

Being able to review a draft of a message for any given Sunday is helpful beyond measure. Now you're glad to have a few more days to think about the suggestions you want to make. *Sorry, Sermon-Sucking Black Hole—no Sunday lunch for you this Mother's Day!*

One Last Thought

I know a photographer who created a wonderful set of worship slides. Everyone liked them. Then she was never asked to do it again. She should have been. After all, since that first success, new ideas have been popping into her head all the time.

More church members than realize it are what I call natural programmers. Ask such a person to find a song that's a good response to a given sermon, and he may have several great suggestions. But here's the really interesting point. Having once done this, for a good while afterward he won't be able to stop thinking about appropriate closing hymns for all the sermons he hears. Sometimes, even when listening to a message, he will reach for a hymnal just to check on the words of a given song to see if they'd fit.

I've noticed the same to be true of those who write or act in dramas. "You know, Pastor," they'll say, "I was thinking about a way what you just preached about could have been put into a short sketch. For example, I picture two people on an elevator…"

But it's frustrating when, oftentimes, these great ideas come during or after the church service. That's why it was so important to me to devise a way that the thrust of a minister's sermon (around which the rest of a worship service is most easily built) could be nailed down early on. Just agree on the sermon subject and the response being called for, and potential "programmers" in the congregation can start working on various service parts even as the minister is finishing writing the sermon.

Chapter 14

The Ultimate Compliment

·······································

I f Jesus visited your congregation in person on a Sunday morning, it's hard to know how people might react. Now we know He's literally there in the Person of the Holy Spirit; He's just not visible to the naked eye. But what if the Lord suddenly appeared in the flesh, right there in the church you attend? What part of the worship service (that you so casually absorb week after week) do you think would become breathtakingly illumined if you could see Jesus with your own eyes?

Upon that first recognition, probably the initial response of many would be one of adoration. Some would drop to their knees. Others might stretch out prostrate before Him. This is the classic body-language of worship. My guess is that before too long a praise song would begin almost spontaneously. What a joy it would be to view with our eyes the response of the One we usually only see by faith.

Imagine what it would be like if the Lord's Table were a part of the service. Perhaps the Lord would actually serve the elements as He did so long ago. The all-too-familiar words, *"This is my body, broken for you ... this is my blood, shed for you..."* would take on powerful meaning. I'm sure a good number in the congregation would declare this the high point of the morning.

Some might say the service came alive in a powerful way at the time of the confessional. When absolution was pronounced, it was as though a great burden rolled off their backs. Think how many people through the ages have longed to hear Jesus say (as He did to the woman taken in adultery), "Your sins are forgiven you. Go and sin no more." What an experience that would be!

The high point might even be during the offering. Giving to Jesus might bring certain people their greatest joy.

How wonderful it might be if you saw Him look directly into your eyes and then felt His hand placed upon your shoulder. Perhaps that might be during an altar call when people were invited to come and "do business" with the Lord.

All this is to say the sermon may not always be the most meaningful part of the service for everyone. But it's usually what the rest of the service is built around if a pastor wants to make the maximum impact on people's lives. So it's worth putting the extra labor into all parts of the service for the potential spiritual meaning to have time to develop.

To the degree that it is frustrating for service-planners to be kept in the dark about the direction of a given Sunday message, it is as commensurately satisfying for them to be told early on the content of the sermon. This is likely your first crack at helping fashion a service using the methodology I'm recommending, so I wanted to make matters as pleasant for you as possible. You were given a whole draft.

Now you have volunteered to come up with two or three suggestions designed to enhance the Mother's Day service.

Number one is a no-brainer: a Scripture card. Unless someone has already been asked, you'll volunteer to take on the responsibility of getting the cards designed and printed, all in time to be inserted in the church bulletins for Mother's Day Sunday.

Suggestion #2 will be a lot more work: finding and displaying pictures of moms. But you believe this is an important way for everyone in the service to identify with his or her own mother, so you decide to request being in charge of putting that package together. You reread your bulletin announcement and make a few small changes:

This year on Mother's Day, Pastor Mains will be preaching about your mom and how to make her happy. Children, youth, adults— find a favorite photo of your mother. Put it in an envelope with your name, address and phone number and leave it at the church office by the final Sunday of April. It will be returned to you. During the Mother's Day service, we want to project pictures of as many of our wonderful mothers as possible and in a way that honors them. You'll be disappointed if yours is missing!

Now, you'll definitely need some help to pull off what you have in mind. But don't ask anyone until you get the pastoral okay on the project.

Would it be best to show these pictures during a musical selection about mothers? What about using a recording? Music is not your strong suit, so you may need assistance. Fortunately, there are many in the church who are skilled in this area.

Suggestion #3 is giving you fits, mainly because you don't know what to call it. In a sense it's like a Scripture reading, but then again it's not. Knowing that the people of the church come from many different backgrounds—positive family experiences and negative ones—after seeing all the pictures you're anxious that no one feel like they were given a far-from-perfect mom. What you want to show from the Bible is that even some of the women we highly revere were at times all too human.

You begin jotting down the names of special women in Scripture, including their flaws. Soon the list gets long, and you decide it's time to attempt to give these thoughts some structure. In the process, you come to the conclusion you are writing a dramatized script for two women readers. Several hours later, still not sure what to call your creation, you've completed a first draft. Is it any good? Let's let the pastor decide.

•••••••••••••••••

A Mother's Day Script for Two Voices

Reader A: Most of the mothers we read about in scripture were Jewish.

Reader B: No Jewish-mother jokes, please!

A: Well, it wasn't exactly a joke that elderly Sarah laughed at. She cracked up over a rather-serious word from God, which wasn't all that appropriate a thing to do.

B: Talk to me when *you're* in your 90s and pregnant. Maybe then you'll appreciate why she's revered in Scripture as the century-long faithful wife of Abraham and the surprise mother of Isaac, the laughing boy.

A: Anyway, these are not perfect mothers we read about in the Bible.

B: No, but they more than adequately filled the role God asked them to play.

A: Like Rebekah, the mother of twins, who had a favorite just like her husband Isaac did, except they each picked a different boy!

B: Everyone knows that having family favorites is a dysfunctional-family trait.

A: And in a number of ways this was a dysfunctional Jewish family.

B: Apparently Rebekah was consistently adequate as a spiritual mom, though, because Jacob turned out to be a man who truly loved the Lord.

A: Remember Job's wife? When life turned sour, she advised her husband to *"curse God and die!"*

B: But she also stuck by her man through thick and thin, and eventually bore him a second set of sons and daughters, of whom it was said, *"Nowhere in the land were there found women as beautiful!"*

A: Rather than throw her new baby in the river as the Egyptians had commanded, Jochebed put a small floating basket containing her young crier out among the reeds of the Nile.

B: She probably felt quite inadequate. Scripture says she had hidden Moses for three terrifying months, but just couldn't do so any longer. Incidentally, the book of Hebrews commends what she did as an act of faith.

A: Ruth wasn't Jewish. But the time came when this young widow from Moab made a critical choice to invest her future with the God of Israel.

B: Little more than a refugee when she arrived in Bethlehem, she would eventually bare a son to rich Boaz. This newborn would turn out to be the grandfather of King David, which placed this Gentile woman in the revered ancestry of Jesus, the future Messiah.

A: If your husband has two wives, I suppose it's to your advantage to be the favorite.

B: But it's to your disadvantage to not be a mother, especially when the rival wife gets pregnant quite easily.

A: A stream of ridicule from the fruitful wife practically made Hannah a basket case. Finally she made a desperate vow to the Lord: "Grant me a son and I'll give him back to You for a lifetime of service."

B: Her impassioned plea was honored by God. And after the child was weaned, true to her word, Samuel was turned over to the service of the Lord.

A: Skipping to the New Testament we soon meet Elizabeth, a good woman only well along in years and still childless.

B: This time it's the husband, Zechariah, who finds a message from God's angel a bit too much to believe. *"I'm an old man,"* he explains to Gabriel, a bit tickled, *"and my wife is well along in years."*

A: Their miracle boy is the future John the Baptist.

B: He's the forerunner of the Anointed of God, Jesus the Christ.

A: Our topic is biblical moms who were less than perfect and yet adequately filled the role God had in mind for them.

B: Remember the overly ambitious mother of James and John? Right before Christ's triumphal entry into Jerusalem, she cornered Jesus and along with her sons knelt before Him with a request.

A: Scripture says the other apostles were furious when they heard what she asked for.

B: *"Grant that one of these sons of mine may sit at your right and the other at your left in your kingdom."*

A: This lady was out to nail down both spots for Johnny and Jimmy.

B: *"You don't know what you're asking,"* Jesus said to the three of them. *"Can you drink the cup I am going to drink?"*

A: There are any number of additional examples we could give, but let's finish with Mary, the mother of Jesus Himself.

B: How does one find fault with her?

A: Well, you get the feeling she and Joseph were a little miffed when after three frantic days of searching, the couple finally discovered their special 12-year-old in the temple courts, sitting with the Jewish teachers. *"Son,"* she snapped, *"why have you treated us like this?"*

B: At the start of our Lord's ministry, He attended a wedding of some family friends. Mary knew Jesus could solve a problem of the house wine having run out. *"Dear woman,"* he cautioned her, *"why do you involve me?"* Not backing off from this motherly pressure on a reluctant son, she informed the servants, *"Do whatever he tells you."* And you know what happened.

A: Perfect mothers—not really.

B: But good moms, and consistently adequate for the task at hand.

A: Each was used by God to accomplish His will,

B: and therefore is a spiritual role-model we still look to today.

• • • • • • • • • • • • • • • •

You decide to call it a "Biblical MOM-tage," and you email it to the pastor with a note about when you'll be calling. You then die a thousand deaths wondering what his response will be!

Finally, the day has come to make the call.

Knowing what it's like to have my creative efforts judged (don't forget that I'm acting as your substitute pastor), I say hello and immediately tell you how much I like the work you've done. I can see how what you've written will not only fit into the morning, but add a missing element. In fact, "I felt good about my sermon. Now I have to work on it some more to make sure it's not overshadowed by other parts of the service."

You feel relieved and grateful, not realizing a minister has just paid you the ultimate compliment. He's suggested that another part of the morning could be even stronger than the sermon!

Dr. Mains: What other dynamite ideas have you come up with? … Yes, if you'd take the Scripture card off of me and run with it, that'd be great … If I encourage the congregation to get in the pictures of their moms, I'm sure they will … Let me talk to the staff about a possible song to use during that time … These repeated ideas will be like rat-a-tat-tats, saying almost the same thing in different ways—rat-a-tat-tat … If I can be of help to you in getting all this done, just holler … This is what the Body of Christ is all about—each of us doing our part. You've done a great job.

After the conversation, you hang up the phone, glowing; it feels so great to have pleased your pastor. More than that, you really are going to be of help to him. Then you suddenly realize this is going to be a ton of work—and you won't be paid a dime—but it's still worth it all. You're glad that your pastor is excited. But if you can hold in your heart the fact that Christ really is present when the congregation of His people bring Him worship and praise—even though you can't see him with your physical eyes—that sense of joy you feel now will be increased to overflowing when you sense that the Lord Himself takes pleasure in your creativity, your willingness to work and your sacrifice of praise. That is even better than the pastor's "good job." Christ's pleasure is the ultimate compliment.

One Last Thought

My first impression was that this *Mother's Day Script for Two Voices* was probably a bit long. Really skilled women readers could pull it off, but if the voices were untrained, there was a good chance the congregation might start to lose interest.

Should I share those feelings?

Not on someone's first attempt to help!

When people step out in faith and volunteer in areas that are new to them, I believe more than anything else, they need to be applauded.

At the same time, participation like this should always be evaluated, just like I believe sermons should be.

Ask, "What did we learn? What might have been done differently? How can we improve the next time?"

People seldom do "their best job ever" the first time they try something. So don't expect instant success.

Churches that now have great drama departments often look back and laugh about their early efforts.

People who do great worship graphics are reluctant to show their first attempts.

For that matter, pastors who sometimes think of re-preaching one of their early sermons often chuckle and admit they find what they did earlier all but useless.

For volunteers to expect early perfection is unrealistic. What's important is that they have a chance to get involved in the process. Hopefully, it won't be for the last time.

Chapter 15

The Joy of Fishing

....

A bout halfway through the writing of this book, I shared some of the early chapters with three friends. I was curious to see if what I felt so strongly about was of any interest to them. One was a minister, the others were not. Two were women, one a man; one older, two younger. Several months later, having heard *nothing* from any of them, I confess I lost some of the enthusiasm that marked me when the writing began.

Coming up on my schedule was a guest spot with the Salvation Army for a three-day officer's retreat. About 100 were to be present, and I was to have 5 sessions. When we first discussed the opportunity, I boldly said my topic would be the Sinister Sermon-Sucking Black Hole. But as the dates drew closer, and I still had no feedback from any of the three friends, I wavered. *This must not be all that interesting a subject,* I thought. I almost phoned to change the theme, but didn't get around to it in the press of things to do.

Packing for the trip, I decided to take notes from other presentations I had done just in case of a last-minute change of heart. Still wrestling matters through on the plane I suddenly had a daring thought. Instead of me preaching at the final session as planned, I would work with someone in the group to be the closing speaker. If that individual grasped what I was saying, incorporated my teaching into their talk, and did a great job, what a marvelous example that would be as to the value of my visit.

I was met at the airport by my host, and we went to lunch, where I shared my idea. He seemed a bit skeptical but didn't disapprove. So I started silently praying, *Lord, lead me somehow to the person You have in mind for this unique assignment.*

Session one went well. The Army is made up of down-to-earth leaders who are open to new concepts as long as they're practical. These men and women had no problem with starting sermon work by nailing down an interesting subject and then a workable response. It's always initially awkward for a group to get used to coming up with "how-tos," but if any organization is "hands-on," it's the Salvation Army. And they also found it challenging to work their way through the "how-long" aspect.

The second session was to be one of exploring several types of Bible passages and seeing how quickly these officers could get their minds around the four key questions regarding each of these texts. In the meantime, I used the break trying to locate the unknown person I was looking for who could speak as taught for session five.

An officer approached me with some questions about his upcoming sermon, and it was quickly clear he understood conceptually what I'd been teaching. His sermon theme also fit the evangelism thrust I'd been assigned for the closing time together, so I felt led to ask if he'd be open to working with me on his Sunday message for that occasion too. His response of "sure" was somewhat matter-of-fact, almost like such requests were commonplace for him. One way or the other, I was relieved to have the matter resolved.

I told the officer in charge the name of the individual I'd picked. His response was less than enthusiastic, and I wondered if I wouldn't be wise to invest some quality time working with the person in his creative process. More than once I've been told, "You believe in people way too much." Maybe I had again leaned too heavily in that direction.

I got back to my volunteer preacher and set up a time to get together. If we skipped a meal, we could put in a couple of hours on this project. He seemed appreciative that the main speaker would give him that much time. Early on we nailed down that his subject would be the joy of fishing. An avid angler, he could think of a good introduction before transitioning to his text. His passage was the well-known account of Jesus telling Peter and Andrew, *"Come, be my disciples, and I will show you how to fish for people."*

Did those in his home corps know how to experience this joy? Probably not, he decided. Why not? The idea of talking to someone else about faith in Christ was intimidating, and they probably weren't sure what that actually sounded like or how to pull it off. Did the Scripture text help with a how-to? Not really.

"Well," I asked, "what are your expectations? After your sermon, do you think your people should be able to actually bring someone through the birthing process of new life in Christ?"

"I doubt whether that's realistic," was his response.

"Then what is it you're expecting of them?"

He couldn't say.

"I'm not a fisherman," I told him. "Obviously you are. Before I invest in the sport, what experience might get me excited about it?"

"Just a couple of nibbles on your line," he answered almost immediately, lifting his eyebrows and nodding his head affirmatively.

"I don't even have to catch anything, just get a few nibbles?"

"That would do it," he assured me. "Fish are smart. They're not as easy to catch as you might think. But a nibble or two makes you aware that they're down there, and that's when the excitement starts … with that first nibble … or two."

"So how do we get your church people to experience the excitement of a spiritual nibble or two on the line?" I asked.

He wasn't sure.

"Okay. Tell me about someone in your congregation—anyone. What does he or she do for a living?"

"Well, there's Ruby. She's a beautician."

"So what if Ruby taped a meaningful Bible verse to one of her shop mirrors, then prayed that a customer would ask her what it was and why it was there. And what if Ruby said it was a truth she was trying to memorize and why it was meaningful to her. Would that be a nibble?"

"Sure, that would be great," he assured me.

We went through similar situations as to what getting a "nibble" would mean for others in his congregation. Then we determined a reasonable amount of time to see this actually happen. Eventually he thought he would be satisfied if there were reports from his people of six nibbles throughout the congregation in, say, the next three weeks.

"So you know your subject," I told him. "Tell me what it is."

"It's the joy of fishing … for fish but also for men … and women."

"And you'll start by talking about the joy you experience when fishing for fish, especially the excitement of that first nibble or two. That opens up your text and the greater thrill Jesus talked about of fishing for people. That's the delight you eventually want your congregation to know. But the how-to for beginners will come in just getting a nibble or two at the start. No nibbles means no fun. And a nibble will be like someone asking Ruby, "What's the thing you have taped on your mirror?" So you're not asking for a boatload of fish in the next day or two. But in three weeks you're looking for reports of some nibbles throughout the congregation. That's your sermon sequence. Everything clear to you? Can you put those thoughts together for me?"

He was confident that he could.

"Read it or preach it to me tomorrow before breakfast," I told him. "In the meantime, I'll start working on some ideas for related service parts like music and Scripture." The truth is, I also had found someone there who was skilled as a mime, and I wanted to see if he could pantomime a fishing scene.

Other contacts were made, and the closing session was coming together. I slept well, and early the last day of the retreat, I met my preaching contact for breakfast to go over his message. He had worked things out well, and with just a few tweaks on my part had a good sermon. "It's shorter than I usually preach," he admitted, "only about 12 minutes, but my people will probably like that."

"So will your fellow officers," I assured him.

"What do you mean?" was his puzzled response.

"When you preach it for today's closing session," I answered.

"When I, uh, do what?" he stammered.

That's when I explained again why I was working with him on this passage. His skin seemed to turn a chalky white. "M-me? I'm preaching the closing session?"

Somehow I guess I hadn't made clear what the arrangement was. So I went over it again, assuring him he would do well. It was then that he rather reluctantly agreed.

I saw him again later that morning. He'd skipped my fourth session to work more diligently on his message. He showed me his changes. He now had twice the material, with more verses, more illustrations and a few quotes—all of which detracted from the clear, elegant direction we'd set earlier. But now, he felt, his peers would be less critical.

We had a long session—the two of us—that finally ended with him agreeing to do it my way. But it was frightening to him. I share the emotion of his struggle only to let you know that ministers have a great fear of being thought of as a "lightweight."

Getting his sermon back to the basic questions needing to be answered, we talked about whether some of his fellow officers at the Salvation Army retreat maybe needed to recapture the joy of fishing like Jesus talked about—and what meaningful nibbles might be in their situations. Then we had prayer, and with no more time for changes, left matters in the Lord's hands.

That afternoon, the elements leading up to the message went very well. The music was right on target, and having the mime just before the message was good—the group enjoyed it, and their laughter helped my volunteer preacher relax. He began his message obviously reliving the joy of fishing, which for him was truly a passion. He described what getting a nibble was like, and whether he knew it or not, he had his audience. Moving to his text was natural, as was the joy he described that Andrew and Peter no doubt experienced as they got ever more into what Jesus had in mind with His challenge.

He segued well into how we could experience this same sense of delight, but cautioned that for some who weren't currently into spiritual fishing, it might take a week or two to recapture the thrill. So he wanted to see if he could help. Explaining what getting a nibble or two would be like for some of his people, he moved into what it might mean for his fellow officers. Finally he gave them a date to remember to check back on whether this had happened. A closing illustration sealed his challenge, and he was done in less than twenty minutes.

My officer looked quizzically at his listeners as if to say, "I know it wasn't all that profound, but anyway, I'm through." Then, as he turned to sit down, everyone in the room rose to their feet and clapped. You would have thought it had been planned ahead of time, but it wasn't. Their applause was spontaneous.

It was one of those times in my life I'll never forget, because it gave me goosebumps. And I thought to myself, *I don't care anymore what those three reviewers thought of my chapters. Maybe they didn't even read them. But what I'm teaching has great value. I know it does!*

Two later events drove this conviction home even more. One was getting a report from the officer's wife that since the retreat, her husband had recaptured the joy of preaching he once knew. The second was a call informing me that my preaching friend had been asked by his divisional commander to travel from his small town post to the big city to preach his "Joy of Fishing" sermon!

Now, I am aware this book is aimed at the concerned lay listener, and you may be thinking, *Nice story, but what does it have to do with me? Maybe I should hand this on to my pastor; he's a great guy, but he really doesn't preach very well.*

The truth is that this chapter, though it is an extended illustration in the life of a Salvation Army minister, is for you as well. Laypeople have all kinds of opportunities to present teachings of various kinds throughout their lives. Indeed, you may be a Sunday School teacher, a small-group leader, even a non-clergy pulpit supply. Much of the teaching of God's Word in the average church is carried on by ordinary, everyday folk who have not been mentored in the skills and lore of public speaking. You, like most, may be terrified of giving platform presentations of any kind to any size of an audience.

These tools are for you. Don't you want your words to be unforgettable in their spiritual impact? I love taking a group of women and mentoring them over a period of weeks in using the four simple sermon-evaluation questions. Often, because of the very fact that they are not seminary-trained, they achieve accessibility in their speaking that I have to work hard to help the professionals achieve.

Please don't hesitate to use this communication tool to improve your own teaching approaches. My prayer is that you, like my Salvation Army friend, will come again to know not only the "joy of fishing" but the thrill of communicating God's principles in life-transforming fashion.

One Last Thought

I have any number of stories like this one. Some are about ordained ministers; others relate to laypeople who have been asked to speak. All of them have a "panic time," when the person involved wonders whether this new approach is going to work.

For clergy, it seems like the four questions go against much of what they've been taught regarding the construction and outlining of messages. For non-clergy, the results don't always sound like the sermons they have been hearing all their lives, and this has a tendency to make them feel insecure.

Making it your first priority to come up with good answers to the questions about subject, response, how to, and how long is a lot harder than it sounds. But the good news is, once this has been done, the rest of the message-making jobs become much simpler. In fact, so much so that the preparation almost seems too easy. That's where the feelings of insecurity come from.

If you are someone who desires to imitate your favorite televangelist, then what I'm advocating is probably not for you. But if you want to get up in front of people and tell them how to be more Christ-like, and to speak with words that are clear and practical and forceful, then what I'm sharing is a pattern you will do well to seriously consider. That's true whether or not your name has a "Rev." before it. And yes, you may gulp a time or two before speaking, but you'll be all right. Trust me.

Chapter 16

Leaving the Sidelines

....

Recently I spoke to a group of about 50 ministers in West Virginia. I drove there instead of flying because I was bringing a carload of materials with me. When the session ended, I loaded my Taurus station wagon with the leftovers and started the eleven-hour drive back to my Chicagoland home.

After a time to mentally debrief the event, I clicked on the radio and hit the "seek" button. The first place it stopped was "Your Country Station." Not much for country-western, I tapped "seek" again. In the hills of West Virginia, the reception must not be very good, because my radio numbers went all across the dial without stopping until they locked on the exact same station. I tried it again with the identical result. So it looked like it was going to be country-western or nothing!

I listened to the first song, about a soldier getting letters from home. It told a story and did it well. Next was a mother's lament because her teenage daughter had run off with the very first guy she fell in love with. Another female vocalist convincingly sold the fact that she was a Redneck Woman and what that meant. After several minutes of commercials, there was a twangy but reflective tune about a husband and wife growing old together. What followed was a musical warning about the tensions always faced when people fall in love. I sensed it was right on target with where a lot of folk are. After about an hour I began to lose the station, but I'd learned a lot. Country songwriters and artists are really good at communicating what's happening in the lives of their listeners. When seminaries are in need of an occasional outside expert, I recommend they bring in someone like Randy Travis or Faith Hill to talk to future ministers about identifying with their audience.

Because that's not going to happen, let me continue in the direction I've been heading. The ideal is an ultimate and ongoing dialogue between pastors and their parishioners. I know firsthand from my ministry in the pastorate, then in religious media, that brainstorming sermon concepts in a team setting creates incarnational communication. Why do I say this? The whole church is the manifestation of the Body of Christ. Men and women, and college kids and oldsters, even little children, are the best living commentary any pastor can access. Good preachers reach into that reality and begin to plumb the untapped resources that are available.

I'm suggesting that in the church, more feedback from listeners is needed if pastors are to learn to communicate with people where they are. Even more, I believe that a regular collaboration between pulpit and pew is the only surefire remedy for the Sermon-Sucking Black Hole. That crucial dialogue has to start somewhere. And because it hasn't happened much at the invitation of ministers, it's probably time for some of you in the congregation to try getting it moving.

When you take that first step toward suggesting some kind of sermon input, you will realize there have been good reasons for determining to build a strong relationship with your pastor. He or she needs to be convinced that you are a true friend and supporter. If it helps, you will also have done the work of contributing to enhancing various parts of the morning service that correlate with the agreed-upon subject of the sermon and the response being called for. Hopefully, in time, this will allow you the opportunity to give greater input into the fashioning of the messages themselves.

I encourage you to participate in what will be an arduous journey before it's finished. When the road feels too long, try to remember there are many good people who have already more or less dropped out of the church. They say it's just not relevant to their worlds. And your heart goes out to seekers who visit but don't return because they find services far-removed from their immediate problems. Even now you have some friends who attend rather sporadically who will probably not be around a year from now if things don't improve. Does what's happening trouble you? Keep on keeping on.

Strange as it sounds, this sense of dissatisfaction can actually be good. Change seldom occurs when people are content with the way things are. A deep sense of unease regarding the state of the church is often the first step in the birthing of revival. But it's important that your dissatisfaction not turn negative. It inevitably will, if you stay on the sidelines. If you let distress sour your prayer effort rather than invigorate your petitions, you will have ceased to play a crucial role in the change that is close to God's heart. That's why I encourage you to actively pursue a place of meaningful involvement.

Do you know that what I'm challenging you to do is not isolated to your church? It's a renewing element that must be repeated countless times and eventually touch tens of thousands of churches before its impact is really felt in this nation.

The reason is that the experiences of people who went to church looking for answers to their problems and left empty are not limited to Methodist churches or Baptist ones. The way disgruntled Catholics talk is not unlike what you hear people say who tried out a Bible church, or a Nazarene or Presbyterian place of worship. Listen to their stories.

A concerned mother: "Our teenage son was accused by a girl at school of touching her inappropriately. There was an immediate suspension, even though he swears such a thing never took place. The school seemed to be in no hurry to sort out what really happened, but the situation was tearing our family apart. Eventually we decided to try going to church. The sermon was about the Apostle Paul writing this letter about Gnosticism. Is that how you pronounce it? I'm not sure I remember what it meant. But then it was like almost the whole service was in a language we didn't really speak, and if we did, I don't think what they said had anything to do with our problem anyway."

Where did they visit that Sunday? Name almost any church group and you're probably right!

An anxious father: "The promotion at work gave us the go-ahead to buy a bigger house and expand the family. No thought was given to a possible company downsizing and the layoff of a lot of middle executives. But that's what happened. Whammo! The severance helped a bit, but it was quickly gone, and the bills just kept coming. I couldn't get a job that paid anywhere near what I'd been making. So what do you do? You try everything—even religion. Two Sundays in church, and all of us came to the conclusion it wasn't for us. The sermon? It was from the Old Testament about a close relative who marries a childless widow and has sex so she can have offspring. Kinsman something. It was related to us and Jesus Christ, but don't ask me how. Our family actually talked about it on the way home. After two times we decided to spend the next Sunday morning at one of those coffee/bookstore places. Yeah, actually found a book that helped some!"

A college sophomore: "I said I'd try it because this guy I kind of like was pushing me about going to his church. What was it like? Lots of singing, then a sermon. The music wasn't exactly my preference. The minister talked about how a church figures out what God wants. What I got was you need to study the Bible a lot. I mean, it wasn't bad or anything. It's just that I probably won't go back. Not right away, anyway."

Think about the youth of our land for a moment. What if a genuine spiritual awakening broke out among young adults across America? I use them as an example because that's the age group in which renewing movements most frequently begin. Say it were to happen through a couple of campus ministries. Then these new converts started attending our churches in large numbers. I hate to say it, but I think our present preaching would kill the movement before it had much of a chance to fan into a bigger blaze!

In fact, I suspect that if the average minister preached the same average Sunday message on a high-school or college campus, or, for that matter, a street corner in town, there wouldn't be many who would stop and listen for long. Am I right or wrong?

It might be revealing at this point to remind us that Jesus did a lot of His preaching in the open air. Scripture tells that He drew great crowds just about everywhere He went. Sure, the miracles were a big reason for His popularity, but the people were also amazed by what He said. His words were reported to have great authority (Matthew 7:28–29). An interesting addendum in that passage is the brief observation that this response was quite unlike the normal reaction given to the teachers of the religious law.

What a tricky time period this was for Jesus to preach in, too. Palestine was an occupied country. Roman soldiers were intentionally visible and large crowds were not something they took kindly toward. Then talk about a topic to speak on over and over—the proclamation of an alternative kingdom or kingship. Our Lord couldn't have chosen a subject more dangerous or more in line with where Jewish thoughts and emotions were.

Jesus was obviously a master communicator who held these huge crowds spellbound and sent them away talking about what He said. He also taught effectively in smaller gatherings, such as the volatile area around the temple in Jerusalem. Often He allowed Himself to be interrupted and comfortably exchanged words with his questioners and/ or opponents. He did a lot of small-group work and one-on-ones. All this is to say that Christ was certainly never isolated from where people were. The common complaints heard about ministers today would never be leveled at this young rabbi:

- too many ideas
- too much spiritual jargon or too theological
- too few illustrations
- too much about the problem, not enough about the solution
- too unrelated to people's lives
- too long
- too boring

When in the synagogues, Jesus made use of the assigned Scriptures for the day, but it's hard to imagine Him in any setting announcing, "Starting this afternoon I want to begin an extended study in the book of Jeremiah." Let's face it, His approach was more country-western topical than it was seminary-trained expositional. He always had a timely word from the Lord, and it certainly resonated powerfully with where the people were living as well.

So the big question facing today's church is, how does it reestablish this Christ-like connection between preacher and people that ensures maximum effectiveness of God's spoken word?

How does the church make certain its message is both God-ordained and on target with where people are living?

How does it build relationships between pastors and parishioners so they can talk honestly and openly about what's helpful and what's not?

How does it show Christian love and respect to God's servants so they don't feel threatened by the process?

How does it at the same time affirm that the best judges of sermons are those who hear and hopefully are helped by them?

How does it bring everyone into agreement about what actually constitutes a good sermon?

How does it learn to treat the sermon as just one key part in a service that's powerful throughout because all the elements work together harmoniously?

And how does it end this sad era of the sinister Sermon-Sucking Black Hole, in which few can recall on Monday what their minister said on Sunday?

One Last Thought

For many people the thought of talking to their pastor about his or her sermon(s) ranks alongside meeting with a representative of the Internal Revenue Service. So let me see if I can help.

You don't want to say, "I'm just not getting anything out of your messages!" Even if that's true, it's a general comment and not very helpful.

I prayerfully prepare for such occasions by having something both affirming and honest that I can say about the pastor's work. Then I move toward the most appropriate of the four questions I've shared time and again. For example, "I understand that last Sunday your subject was people who live in a fantasy world. But I was confused as to how you wanted me to respond to your sermon."

If the response was clear but the "how to" was not, I would say, "I know you commented briefly in your sermon that you wanted us to trust God more, but you didn't develop that thought at all. In my situation I'm not clear as to what 'trust God more' means. Could you be more specific?"

Questions like these are much easier to deal with because they keep the conversation confined to something manageable. If the exchange is positive they also help your pastor better understand how his or her messages relate to your world. And who knows—such meetings could eventually lead to discussing the sermons before they are preached!

Chapter 17

We're Not Perfect,
But We're Making Progress

···

"No one is perfect like Jesus," the minister told his attentive congregation. He was underscoring his point that we all need to be less critical and more forgiving. "Let me see the hands of any here who are without sin. You reckon you have reached perfection." He encouraged people to "lift them high so all can notice." There were no takers.

Pressing the point, the man of God next inquired, "Has anyone here ever *met* somebody like Jesus? You know, a contemporary individual who never does anything wrong. Never sins. Again, let me see a show of hands."

To his great surprise, one arm appeared to be partially raised. It didn't shoot up all the way, but there it was, bent and maybe halfway extended, from a right-side pew about a third of the way back. The minister couldn't pretend to not notice; the arm was just high enough that many could see it. And goodness, it was old George Brakenridge—a quiet, unassuming gentleman. This was certainly a surprise. Maybe he just hadn't heard right.

The minister looked kindly toward him and now spoke in a voice a little below his normal preaching tone. Slowly, clearly enunciating each word, he said: "I am asking, Brother Brakenridge, whether anyone here knows someone, or has met a person, who is perfect like Jesus Christ. Now, did you intend to raise your hand indicating you have?"

"Well, I can't honestly say I actually met this fellow," was the soft-spoken reply. "But..." There was a definite pause. "...but from all my wife tells me about him, I'd say it's quite possible that her first husband was perfect."

This chapter is for all of you who realize you have less-than-perfect pastors. And just to set the record straight, less-than-perfect pastors can't be expected Sunday after Sunday to preach 100% perfect sermons, sermons that fit into well-themed and creatively beautiful services, services that are sure to satisfy everyone regardless of age or spiritual maturity. To hold to such an expectation would be as unfair as the new Mrs. Brakenridge all-too-frequently mentioning the idealized memory of her deceased first husband.

I sincerely hope what I have written in this small book will not set up unrealistic expectations. To make sure you understand my point, it is dead wrong to assume that by implementing my simple suggestions, your church will do an instant about-face. I don't believe for one minute it will suddenly and remarkably manifest characteristics that are the exact opposite of those churches afflicted by the Sermon-Sucking Black Hole.

Were the perfect minister, Jesus Himself, to take on the role of pastor for your congregation, I'm sure there would still be some on Monday morning who wouldn't be able to remember the subject of His sermon from the day before.

Not that our Lord wouldn't make it clear. Of course He would. For example, let's say He preached a reworked version of His famous "Sermon on the Mount," in Matthew 5–7. Listeners should be able to quickly nail down that His subject was the lifestyle of those who identify with the Kingdom of God. You'd expect most in attendance to give an answer like, "He talked about how those who bow before Him as King should live."

The desired response of our Lord would be that listeners submit to His teachings. Hopefully, His listeners would be wise, hearing and also obeying Him, responding like those who build their house on a sure foundation, which stands secure even when the storms of life beat upon it. Remember the ending illustration our Lord used in His "Sermon on the Mount"?

On their own, would people be able to put what Jesus taught into practice? Could they just stop worrying, or judging, or committing adultery (both physical and mental)? I assume Jesus' updated sermon would include some helpful "how-tos" and "how-longs." But it still doesn't mean that everyone hearing Him preach would immediately fall in line behavior-wise. Even perfect pastors still have to cope with less-than-perfect parishioners.

With this in mind, let me next see if I can spell out the kind of incremental changes I envision in those individuals concerned about church change. These thoughts relate to the start of, say, a five-year program of improvement. For examp—

"Five years!" someone interrupts with a loud sigh. "Did I hear you say 'five years'? To me, that sounds like an eternity. I'm not sure I can last for five more years!"

"That's too bad," I reply, "because that's probably about how long it's going to take for your church to start to arrive at where it needs to be. But hear me out. What may sound like forever to you is really quite short when you're referring to ecclesiastical changes. *In church work you have to learn the secret of getting to where you want to go as fast as you can as slowly as possible!"*

So here are a dozen indications that to me would say early progress is truly being made (this is the personal work you must begin with if you are concerned about the Sermon-Sucking Black Hole).

1. You are regularly praying for your pastor, and your requests are not as surface as they once were.
2. You are learning to see your minister through the loving eyes of Jesus and are starting to understand what Christ saw in this person when He challenged him or her to church work. And you affirm the wisdom of that divine call.
3. You are taking notes during the church service. Even when the four simple questions—subject?, response?, how to?, how long?—are not addressed in the sermon, you attempt to come up with appropriate answers on your own.
4. You are quick to personally affirm what's done well by your pastor, and are also praying about how to constructively address where skills can be improved.
5. You are working at building a positive relationship, making certain your pastor knows you are a supportive team member.
6. You are actively searching each Sunday for how God speaks TO you during the main service of the church.
7. You are also searching each Sunday for how God can consistently speak THROUGH you to others when the congregation comes together.
8. You are making sure you TALK ABOUT what God says TO and THROUGH you in the Sunday worship service.

9. You are able to name specific ways you've observed the sermons and services improve, and you are less critical and more forgiving in your attitude about what goes on.

10. You are positive regarding the future of the church and can envision specific improvements three, six, nine, or twelve months from now.

11. You are starting to work on a list of individuals you want to invite to a church service sometime in the future.

12. You are no longer thinking about dropping out or going elsewhere, but instead are doing all you can to make your present church experience the best it can possibly be.

These could be good year-one indications to you that significant change is taking place. They fall a long way short of perfection, but that's not really something you need to concern yourself with during this lifetime.

Before long I would also hope to see some of the following signs surfacing in terms of the rest of the congregation:

1. People are picturing themselves more as participants in the services than before, and a few are starting to regularly pray about what goes on.

2. People are improving in their group singing. They are certainly more conscious of the words to the songs, and to whom they are addressed.

3. People are definitely noticing a difference in the way the sermons are preached. For example, more references are now being made to the everyday world of the members of the congregation.

4. People are also conscious of a stronger connection between the spoken word and the rest of the service.

5. People are now emotionally involved in the Sunday services. It is not infrequent to notice tears in evidence.

6. People are staying around longer after the service and not just rushing to leave. A few individuals even remain in the sanctuary, prayerfully processing what they heard.

7. People are more complimentary in their after-service remarks. They affirm the preaching, as well as other elements of the worship experience.

8. People are appreciating being asked for their input regarding the Sunday experience. Even if they don't get personally involved, they feel good having been extended the opportunity.

9. People are frequently talking throughout the week about the Sunday service or sermon, and most of what is said is positive.

10. People are aware of recent spiritual victories in their lives. Though they are still far from perfect, they are at least able to specify how they have made positive changes in recent months.

11. People are more serious about their faith than they were previously. This is not true of everyone, but it certainly is of a significant number.

12. People are obviously more excited about their church than they used to be. Some have actually invited friends and neighbors to attend with them.

Admittedly, these affirmations are not what most would envision as a church at the extreme opposite of the Black Hole. We're not talking yet about weekly conversions, Christ-like love permeating the Body, worship that's enjoyed by both the people and the Lord, powerful and practical preaching, spiritual and numerical growth, meaningful and vital fellowship, a deep concern for the nations of the world, a marvelous sense of well-being, plus—I almost forgot—many people actually remembering on Monday what the minister preached on Sunday!

The point I'm making is to not be discouraged if everything doesn't happen all at once. It's going to take some time. There's a "how long" factor to be considered. So yes, keep your eyes focused on the ultimate. But along the way, be encouraged that certain incremental steps are being made.

Keep praying for all that God has in mind, but also recall the good minister's point, "No one is perfect like Jesus, therefore we all need to be less critical and more forgiving—of others, yes, and also of ourselves."

One Last Thought

One of my closest friends is a skilled orthodontist. He creates beautiful smiles for people, but it takes a lot of time. The nature of his work is such that he can't be rushed. Offer him twice as much money to do the job in half the time and he'll just laugh.

Many small adjustments take a long while to add up—years, to be more precise. I'm one who is also convinced of this. A lifetime of church experiences has forced me to accept a snail's pace as often being reality in religious settings.

You believe a pastor finally understands how important "how-tos" are, and you're honored when he asks you to come and hear him preach. But his sermon has nothing that even remotely resembles a "how-to." *Okay, we can meet and go over it again. But Lord, did he have to publicly thank me for all the help I've supposedly been giving him?*

Patience is a biblical virtue. It's one of the *"fruit[s] of the Spirit"* Paul lists in Galatians 5:22. Keep this in mind because, if you're someone from a congregation who God has called to help change His church, there's a good chance your patience will be tested time and again. Just remind yourself that the nature of this work is such that it can't be rushed, not without negative consequences.

Slow but relentless—move the teeth a little bit at a time—tighten this band one more half-turn—and remember how good the smile will be when all the ivories are perfectly aligned!

Chapter 18

Partners in Sermon- and Service-Planning

···

I t's interesting to me that during my lifetime, the person the media bestowed the title of *"the Great Communicator"* upon was not a preacher but a politician. Ronald Reagan used television to talk to Americans as though he was sitting with them in their homes. Even when addressing massive crowds, he employed this same friendly, low-key, straightforward approach. But our 40th President firmly believed it was his ideas, not his manner, that captured the hearts of his hearers. In his farewell address he said, "I never thought it was my style or the words I used that made a difference; it was the content."

People who followed Reagan's career know he was for fewer government regulations, lower taxes and a strong military. He also was held an optimistic belief in the goodness of America and the principles that made her great. Reagan demonstrated an amazing ability to inspire people, but you'd never say he sounded like a preacher! In fact, it's hard to picture Ronald Reagan talking to the American public while shaking his fist and pacing back and forth in the style of your typical televangelist! Is there a preacher "sound"? I've known so many different ministers, it's hardly fair to categorize them as one. But you and I both know the stereotype: a lot of hollering without much reasoned thought. This old-fashioned sawdust trail style can be entertaining for those raised on it, but it seems an outdated, rather pompous delivery style to those not accustomed to it. The traditional 3-point outlines are often alliterative—each point begins with the same letter or sound—making a listener feel like everything just reverted back to the 1800s. It's marked by stories, humor and an occasional poem, but the bottom line is unclear (unless it's an altar call for salvation). It's flashes of rhetorical eloquence plus (in certain traditions) excessive sweating—and critics might add, an annoying way of talking down to people in a way that implies they're less intelligent, and certainly less spiritual.

Sounding preachy is not a compliment. Morgan Spurlock, the director and human guinea-pig of the movie *Super Size Me*, in which he documented the effect on his body of eating McDonald's fast food exclusively for 30 days, credits the success of his documentary by saying, "We present things in a way that's not preachy or chastising."

Regardless of the niche audience watching religious television, I believe the days of the "spellbinding preacher" are a thing of the past. There has been a paradigm shift in our land. Reagan was right: The substance of what's said has to ring true if you want people to listen for long. The key to great spoken communication is compelling content.

I fear much of the contemporary American church has placed too high a value on excessive emoting. It seems it doesn't much matter what's said, as long as it's presented passionately. If you expect to move people, make it obvious you feel strongly about your message. Use your body more—wave your arms, pace back and forth across the platform, even go down into the audience and talk loudly if need be. You must excite people. Make sure they respond somehow, say "amen" now and then, at least applaud once in a while.

Agreed, being dull about a word from the Lord is dreadful. Passion is fine—but not when it comes at the expense of content!

Don't get me wrong. By compelling content I don't mean profundity or an emphasis on deep and esoteric truths. The point of a sermon can be quite simple, as long as it speaks to where people struggle to grow and rings of authenticity. What's beautiful is that the truths of God's Word are in and of themselves both captivating and attractive. If presented clearly, they can be almost irresistible to those seeking ultimate meaning.

My wife, Karen, once attended a weekend seminar sponsored by the University of Chicago; they were in a two-year project of mounting the medieval "Mystery Cycle" plays. Produced in cathedral cities like York, these presented the panorama of Scripture, from Satan's expulsion out of heaven to the Last Judgment. These dramatic events were a way the church (sponsored by various guilds in the town) could tell the biblical accounts to a population that was mostly illiterate. Sometimes the Mystery Cycles could take as long as 24 hours to dramatize. The modern presentation in Chicago divided the stories in half, ending the first year at the nativity of Christ, with the gospel accounts and the birth of the Church to be told the following year.

The stories, strung together in an audience-participation fashion called ambulatory theatre, sought to recall the Mystery Cycle tradition of England in the Middle Ages. "Found objects" were used for the actors' costumes the way guild members once used tools and props common to their trades—for instance, in the Chicago production, God made His proclamations (taken from Genesis) wearing a workman's overalls, a hard hat, and rising above the stage in a cherry-picker. The angel Gabriel appeared, his wings made from the translucent plastic rings of beer six-packs, stapled together.

Karen said that amazingly, the Scripture stories began to take on the feeling of transcendence, acted out admittedly by skilled improvisational actors from Chicago's world-renown Second City theatre. They used their professional experience to involve that part of the audience seated in bleachers on the sanctuary platform. Yet, the scholar who translated the Mystery Cycle texts from the Old English was a liberal or nominal Christian at best; the producer, a well-known theatre director, was Jewish; and certainly most of the crew and players had no literacy in Scripture. We can accurately surmise that the pieces were not being mounted with a propagandist agenda in mind.

Yet, the next day, Karen reported intriguing discussions with the weekend workshop attendees, most of whom were University of Chicago graduates. The Jewish producer announced, amazed, that before mounting this Cycle, he had never understood that the Hebrew story of Abraham sacrificing Isaac prefigured the Christian story of God allowing His Son to be sacrificed for the world. Quite a profound leap of understanding.

One woman, a teacher at an exclusive private school, said to the group, "I'm an atheist. I came this weekend because I teach English and the Bible as literature. But when those actors, during the Nativity story, began to pass out the lit candles to the audience so we could hold them up to show that the Light had come into the world, I thought to myself, 'If they don't give me one, I'm liable to *kill* for it!'"

Karen came home from that weekend convinced that the story we have is powerful if we will just tell it. Conservative Christians would not have trusted that unbelieving crew to mount these sacred stories; sometimes in our seriousness, we drain the Scripture of its mystery and delight. These secular professionals, however, having no agenda to push, found the beauty in the meaning that is there, were slightly irreverent and thereby disarmed their audience, and consequently the message spoke forth even more powerfully to unsuspecting spectators because there was no attempt to persuade them.

Sometimes I think we Christians work too hard to get our message across because we don't believe it has power to change lives. We have lost our trust in the Bible and the power of the Holy Spirit to apply its truth. Consequently, we feel that we have to do the convicting, have to speak forcefully, and have to be intellectually erudite.

We need to develop a communication system simple enough to let the Bible speak for itself. We must be careful that our style and delivery and outline don't get in the way of the truths we are proclaiming. That is one reason I have worked so hard through the decades to develop a methodology simple enough to not interfere with the meaning of the Word, let alone to be applicable to both novices and professionals.

I contend that the average minister, trained to preach a certain way, on their own will never be a great communicator with compelling content. Not that there can't be exceptions; I've met some remarkable preachers who, from all I can tell, are quite self-sufficient, using the best of their training and discarding what is no longer useful (often these preachers began their lives in other professions and are more in touch with the listening needs of their audiences). But my remarks refer to the *average* minister, the ones most of you have serving in your church. They need your help. If you can learn to offer that to your pastor in a way that it can be received, I believe his or her ministry will be enhanced, and trusting in that powerful content, enhanced by a simple four-question methodology, framed out of dialogue with members of the congregation, before long your preacher will also be above-average. If he or she is above-average now, the potential for being exceptional is ahead.

What's needed on the part of ministers is a new conviction that the people listening are capable of determining how valuable a given sermon is to them. Pastors should also start to view their hearers as an important resource in the whole of the preaching process—before, during, and after a message is given.

The congregation, including individuals like you, must cease being passive and, supportively as possible, show a much greater interest and involvement in both sermons and services. Stop assuming there's little you can do to contribute to or change them.

When moving to more of a partnership in sermon preparation between the podium and the pew, the first step in the transition is undoubtedly the hardest. It's developing an easy rapport between a pastor and various congregants that allows for open discussion regarding the messages. That's why it's often helpful to start by talking about other parts of the service. These aren't quite as personal to the minister as the sermon, and they allow the clergy to critique what others do before the process starts to include their role.

Is there a danger that over time those invited into the process of evaluating what's said from the pulpit might develop a critical attitude? It's possible, but more likely, these individuals will start to develop a valuable discerning spirit. When any of us are invited into a process, when our ideas are respected, when we feel that what we do and say is valuable, believe me, ownership grows rapidly. When I conducted weekly sermon- and service-brainstorm groups in my congregation, almost all the assignments for research, or for special approaches to service segments, were joyfully and willingly picked up by the people in the brainstorm group. More remarkably, I can't think of one time in ten years when anyone assigned a task out of the idea sessions let me down.

My laypeople did good work to the best of their ability. I did check in to see how they were doing, or to offer help if they needed it, but most of the time, what they created went beyond what I as a professional could've done. That is why I'm convinced you, the layperson, have exceptional gifts and understanding to bring to this whole process, and when those gifts are exercised carefully and wisely, they will eventually bring about stunning results. Not only will laypeople remember on Monday what was preached on Sunday, they'll be talking about sermon and service ideas on Wednesday! I promise.

Because of my media involvement, I haven't been in a local church pastorate for over 30 years, but people still run into me, decades after a service, eager to report, "Remember that Sunday when you preached on (here they repeat a preaching-summary sentence almost verbatim)? You were in the middle of a series on 'The Christian, the Church, and Society.' You handed out response cards to put in our Bibles and check off how we were doing in certain areas. I still have that card. That series changed my life."

Please understand, I know that I am not one of the world's greatest preachers. However, when I have trusted my parishioners for input, when I have gone to my staff teams for feedback, I am aware that a certain memorability begins to engage what I say. Since most sermons can't pass the "get-past-the-parking-lot" test, think how I must feel when I have regularly had people quote back to me the subject and the response of sermons I preached decades ago. Frankly, it makes me feel pretty good.

The benefits of lay brainstorm teams are almost innumerable, but let me mention two others. You as laypeople will begin to appreciate more and more the careful thought that goes into anyone presuming to speak on God's behalf. You will become party to your pastor's labor, to the agony of the soul that happens when communicators struggle to speak truth in an authentic way. You will also begin to bear the burden of speaking the Word. I can't imagine a minister not thanking God for this kind of caring team. In addition, you'll begin to understand the distress that comes from working hard, working carefully—and being criticized, being misunderstood by someone in the congregation who takes the innovative offering you created in the wrong way. This kind of empathy for what a pastor often endures week after week is invaluable to them.

In our day, it's unlikely that any minister will steal *"the Great Communicator"* title from Ronald Reagan and his team. I added "and his team" because presidents have speechwriters who help craft the many talks they're asked to give. A chief executive doesn't personally script every Saturday radio visit, fundraising speech or State of the Union Address. They're vitally involved in the process, but it's also true that some of our leaders' greatest lines were originally penned by someone else. These are professional writers who are paid handsomely to make the President sound articulate and profound.

While having a salaried writing team has its advantages, pity the poor President whose speeches get instantly analyzed on network TV by political commentators of all stripes. Pastors are fortunate not to conclude a sermon only to have several parishioners rush to the platform to express their varied opinions before the closing hymn even begins!

Few congregations would seriously consider having a team of speechwriters for their pastor anyway. But this doesn't mean parishioners can't be regularly involved in helping fashion sermons. Obviously some people's input will be more valuable than others' (though I have been often amazed at the ideas that come from the very ones I prejudged to be less apt). If you as a layperson begin to put planning teams together for your pastor, don't overlook people you may have prejudged; it's immensely beneficial discovering what *any* church member finds meaningful.

Again, this caution is in order: This is not a problem that will be solved over a couple of weeks by a few simple tweaks. I am personally 100% convinced, however, that preachers will not be able to resolve their preaching dilemmas strictly on their own. Without regular input from the congregation, reading my words and even changing their approach to sermon-preparation will still not result in the optimum retention from people in the pews. That is achieved when pastors realize they desperately need more feedback from their listeners and begin to put a process in place where that can be achieved.

I'm also not sure whether the average listener can be patient enough and gracious enough and honest enough to stick with the process I've described in this short book. So admittedly, what I'm recommending will be a rather long journey of walking together before achieving the desired end. Like a dysfunctional marriage where the problems have been created by both parties, it takes a while just to be able to hear one another out and to start to recognize what's true and what isn't.

But somewhere in the weeks and months and (yes) years ahead, a bonding should take place. Preachers will begin to truly value what you their listeners have to say. You, representing the parishioners, will not only share your input, but before long you and everyone else should start to recall a lot more from the sermons you hear. Because of this, the compelling content of God's Word will soon manifest itself in the lives of His people.

Once that happens, it won't be long before the sinister Sermon-Sucking Black Hole loses its gravitational pull and evaporates, becoming a thing of the past!

The intriguing and dramatic history of the discovery of black holes is delineated in *Empire of the Stars: Obsession, Friendship, and Betrayal in the Quest for Black Holes*, by Arthur I. Miller. The author reveals how in 1935 a shy, almost boyish but brilliant Indian astrophysicist rose to address the Royal Astronomical Society in London.

Dr. Subrahmanyan Chandrasekhar, only 24 years of age, presented a mathematical solution (which finally in the 1960s was verified as accurate) that proved stars collapsed upon themselves at the end of their lifecycles (forming black holes). This flew in the face of all the accepted tenets of the science of stars known at that time and was a completely new concept, original to this young man.

This paper was ruthlessly savaged by the world's then-greatest astrophysicist, Sir Arthur Eddington, consequently setting the stage for the drama that continued over decades and which is examined in Arthur I. Miller's book. He writes:

> Only one person understood the full implication of Chandra's discovery: Sir Arthur Stanley Eddington. ... Eddington himself had flirted with the idea that a dead star might collapse indefinitely in this manner, so he should have been delighted with Chandra's mathematical declaration. Instead, he used a meeting of the Royal Astronomical society to savage Chandra's result cynically and unmercifully. The encounter cast a shadow over the lives of both men and hindered progress in astrophysics for nearly half a century.

It is past time for us to come to terms with the general lack of effectiveness in the transforming power of the Sunday worship service and the weekly sermon event. Without being reckless, we professional clergy nevertheless must be prepared to discard old methods of communication no longer appropriate for the listeners of our times.

"They have ears to hear, but do not hear" is not only the problem of the hearer; it is a lack of willingness to change, which is too often endemic to the proclaimers of the Word. Tragically, this is not necessary. It is imperative to think outside the box regarding the way preachers communicate and how the solution to solving the obstacles to effective preaching lies in pastor/parishioner collaboration. For the sake of hungry souls, we cannot afford to set the cause of Christ back half a century. Let's put the design teams together that are best equipped to find the solutions to this communication conundrum.

One Last Thought

Which of these two approaches seems to you to be the better one?

1. "I've read that some ministers find it helpful when preparing their sermons to early on discuss their ideas with a member of their congregation. I just wanted to let you know that if you wanted to try that, I would be willing to volunteer."

   OR

2. "I've read that some ministers find it helpful when preparing their sermons to early on discuss their ideas with a member of their congregation. I just wanted to let you know that if you wanted to try that, I would be willing to volunteer once or twice."

Most clergy I know would respond that the second option is the better of the two. It doesn't mean your pastor can't decide later to ask for your help beyond the initial two meetings. But it does mean that the preacher has a gracious way to stop the process of it doesn't appear to be working all that well.

All you're doing is reversing roles and discovering the value of the "how-long" element regarding what you have to say.

"What if my pastor asks me where I heard that ministers were early on discussing their sermons with congregation members like this?" you ask.

Naturally, you just give your pastor a copy of *The Sermon-Sucking Black Hole*.

And as long as we're working with the "how-long" question, say that you'll stop by to pick it up again in a week!

Chapter 19

Laughter, Creativity
and Productivity

··

E nough was enough. He'd obviously had it. You could tell he felt pressured to be in church far more than what his mind figured was reasonable. So, during the service he slowly stood to his feet on one of the front pews, where he had been quietly seated next to his family. Then he suddenly turned around, faced the congregation, and announced in his loudest voice, "I hate church!"

If he had been older, people probably would have been shocked. Instead, they laughed ... and laughed ... then paused and laughed some more. Coming from a 4-year-old, it just sounded funny. That young Master Rhett was the pastor's boy only added to the humorous incongruities of the situation. Craig, the minister and my brother-in-law, still chuckles when he tells this story.

The truth is, there are probably adults who would like to replicate his son's poignant declaration. They're just too inhibited to voice their frustrations in quite as public a manner. Unfortunately, most of them have little or no awareness that they could play a key role in bringing about a solution to whatever it is that's troubling them.

If the church services are being criticized, my experience convinces me that these won't improve much if the pastor is the only individual working to solve the problem. It will take the involvement of a large number of worshipers to pull off what needs to be done. By now, my readers should know that I don't believe those who do little more than attend church on weekends have the luxury of lambasting sermons or services as though the problem had nothing to do with them. I've stated repeatedly my conviction that on their own, most ministers really don't have the wherewithal to resolve these matters. To preach with maximum impact pastors need significant input from their people. Planning powerful services is also too big a task for the professionals to try to go it on their own.

What consistently bogs down the collaborative process, or what makes it harder than it should be to work together, is the difficulty of determining with enough lead time what is an unchanging bottom-line. That's because the way most ministers have been trained to create sermons, they don't get to that part—if they ever do—until quite late in their preparation. And without something to build on as basic as the sermon's subject and response, how can the rest of the service be themed all that well?

It's not enough for a pastor to say, "Any Christmas music will do. I mean, it's December, isn't it?" I've been in too many Advent services where singing carols before or after a sermon actually detracted from what was preached. The familiar words and music went in a direction that had nothing to do with what the Holy Spirit was speaking to people about through the preached word. Otherwise, the song was sung but not really entered into, and the congregation might just as well have joined together on "Silver Bells" as far as any meaningful connection was concerned.

But now open yourself to an exciting truth. Once there are agreed-upon standards, and these start being consistently worked with, progress can be quite rapid. In fact, with agreement on how to evaluate what's happening, agreement that allows for flexibility regarding personalities, the whole process of preparing sermons and services is far less time-consuming, and get this—it's actually exciting, not to mention quite a bit of fun!

As a professional, I've observed planning meetings where almost nothing was accomplished the whole first hour. Asked if I had any suggestions, I quickly focused on getting clear answers regarding the sermon subject and response. With just these two points nailed down, plus what a related worship theme might be, the meeting suddenly took on new life. So many ideas were shared, there was carryover for future Sundays. The group's demeanor changed from confusion to clarity, from struggle to excitement, from work to play. All this tells me you just have to believe in and work the system.

There's a huge difference between a group coming together to work on "the present preaching series we're in on Hebrews" compared to being told, "My sermon subject will be *God's Phenomenal Gift of the Conscience*, and the response called for in this 1 Peter 3:16 passage is to *keep it clear.*"

"So," someone could wonder, "where do you come up with a hymn about the conscience?" Though there aren't that many pieces written about this topic, some can be found. Besides, what prohibits a layperson with the gift of wordsmithing from writing new lyrics to be sung to a familiar hymn tune?

Think about the unique gift of a working conscience given to all humans. What is it about God that deserves His people's praise? That

He is a marvelous Creator? That He is a Master Communicator who comes up with ingenious ways of getting our attention? That through the Holy Spirit, He frequently makes His presence felt through our conscience? That His truth is what beautifully starts to program the new believer's tender conscience? All kinds of worship examples could work here, but you get the idea.

What are occasions during the week when attendees might sense their conscience coming into play? For example, taking a test, watching television, writing a résumé, talking on the phone, making a sale. These, and numerous other situations, could easily form the basis for a short drama.

Are there Scriptures that could be read, juxtaposed against a familiar movie scene involving the conscience, such as the masterful scenes of Gollum's schizoid back-and-forth musings in the *Lord of the Rings* series?

What negative examples might be tapped into that would reveal the tragedy of a seared conscience? For me, a student of Shakespeare, lines lifted from the musings of a guilty and murderous Macbeth and the nighttime sleep walking of his maddened Lady, are classic examples of the results of a guilty conscious.

Try a "Finish This Sentence" approach: *Lord, if You hadn't made me with a conscience...* Explain in the church bulletin that during the morning prayer, worshipers will be asked to complete this short statement.

Is this starting to seem like fun? I hope so, because it should be.

What's not fun is being in a Sunday-is-rapidly-approaching scenario and trying to figure out what will seem meaningful to people in a service where the basic sermon ingredients are still up in the air. After all, isn't Friday a little late to begin deciding what worship elements best enhance the sermon? The truth is, the largest sermon Web site in the country reports that the majority of hits they receive are from preachers on Saturday!

People lead busy lives. To give up several prime evening hours every week or two to brainstorm church services is a major commitment. Heading home with an additional assignment to accomplish usually tacks on several more hours of creative work to a lay-person's week. Yet when the involvement is exciting, when gifts are being used, the extra labor is never viewed as a sacrifice. Volunteers invariably look forward to participating.

You know your group is well into the process of positive change when laughter, creativity and productivity marks the evenings. Conversely, you know you're *not* working the system the way you ought to if most of the night is spent "wheel-spinning." You're not really getting anywhere in service-planning, and probably because there aren't clear answers to the first two simple questions about the sermon subject and response.

Learning new skills can be frustrating, especially in the early stages. A harmonica doesn't look very intimidating when you first examine one. You can even make pleasant notes on it on the first try. But making it sound like something a friend would eventually want to hear you play will take time and work. Learning from a good teacher should hurry up the process, so you take lessons. Somewhere down the line you turn a corner, and suddenly it's like, "What do you know, this is fun!" Well, this happens in sermon- and service-planning too. When it does, it's like you want to stand on a chair or a pew and yell to everyone around, "I love church!"

One more thought: A habit is a behavior pattern acquired by frequent repetition. Which do you think is more difficult to break—a good habit or a bad one? Most people guess the answer is a bad habit. They focus on a problem, like trying to stop smoking. But the truth is, all habits are hard to break. Brush your teeth every morning (a good habit), and it will be tough to convince yourself to skip it for a while. Another positive example, if you attend church every Sunday for (say) a decade, you'll find it next to impossible to sleep in on a given weekend. A habit is a habit.

What I've been trying to do for you as a reader is to get you into the habit of every Sunday looking for the answer to four simple questions—subject? response? how to? how long?—every time you listen to a sermon. Sure, there are many other aspects related to good message-preparation and delivery. But you don't have to worry about them. Preaching is not your expertise. All you need is an easy way to evaluate what you hear and give helpful feedback as to whether it's helped you become a better Christian.

I should add that if you are part of a service-planning group, you also need a quick way to come up with what the worship theme will be. Remember again, my primary target audience for this book is not preachers; it is you who listen to sermons Sunday after Sunday, month after month, and year after year.

My desire in sharing the basics of what I've learned through a lifetime of work in this field includes the bonus of wanting to wrap the more-functional aspects of service-planning with an element of joy … of delight … of celebration. For it to be what it should be, unadulterated pleasure needs to eventually show up in both the planning of services as well as their execution.

This doesn't necessarily mean that what you do will be easy. Mastering any skill or gift always takes a certain amount of sweat. But in time you should realize, *I'm getting quite good at this, and that's bringing me joy. It's not that I'm cocky, and I'm always aware of my dependence upon the Lord, but that said, my input into problem-solving the Sermon-Sucking Black Hole has become extremely valuable. The help I give truly makes our worship services better, including even the sermons, and that's touching lives now in a remarkable way. How wonderful! Thank You, Jesus. I know we haven't arrived as a church, but I believe we're turning a corner, and does that ever feel good!*

New approaches always meet with resistance. Let's anticipate that, particularly when there hasn't been time to test what seems a radical idea. Arthur I. Miller states that, until the proof of their existence became irrefutable, much of the resistance to black-hole theory was because most physicists considered the possibility of black holes' presence to be "ugly, ungainly objects that spoiled a harmonious universe." However, after decades of research building upon its own foundations, after the splitting of the atom and the resultant destructive bombs (the core of a hydrogen bomb resembles nothing so much as an exploding star), after more sophisticated measuring and viewing approaches were developed, teams of eager scientists (among whom was Subrahmanyan Chandrasekhar) began to make the connections between the structure of black holes, electromagnetism, and gravitational waves. Black holes were considered to hold the answers to the mystery of the universe, pushing mankind's knowledge of the cosmos to the limits.

Black holes, instead of "ugly, ungainly objects spoiling the perceived harmony of the universe," are now, in Chandrasekhar's words, seen as "the most perfect macroscopic objects there are." This astrophysicist consequently suggests, after all these decades of laborious scientific research, that we learn to stand "shuddering before the beautiful."

Let us not close ourselves off to new ideas, no matter how strange they may seem. Certainly let us not negate them before they have been tested. The Sermon-Sucking Black Hole may be a tool that in God's hands will force us to consider a wholly new approach to sermon-preparation and service-planning, an exciting collaboration between pastors and laypeople that will help us Sunday after Sunday "shudder before the beautiful."

One Last Thought

It's fun to be a part of something that is working really well. The overall objective is clear, people understand their various roles, relationships are harmonious, a sense of enthusiasm permeates the endeavor, and goals are not only met, but regularly surpassed.

By way of contrast, it's also obvious when something isn't working the way it should. Basic goals aren't being met, people start to get testy, they tend to get in each other's hair, negative comments are common, efforts are more of a grind, and there's considerable disagreement about purpose.

There's little question as to which of these paragraphs you want to be descriptive of your church. Which one actually is, could be a different matter.

One of the clear signs that things are at least headed in the right direction is an overall sense of joy in what is happening. All things being equal, one would expect the presence of Christ to infuse such a setting with His joy. Was it fun to be around Jesus when He was healing the sick, performing miracles and preaching about the Kingdom? Of course it was! Is it fun to be involved in His church when it's functioning the way it was intended? Obviously so!

Jesus is a most sympathetic friend in our sorrows and griefs, but He's also great to have around when celebrations are the order of the day. And who can think of a better reason to celebrate than when a church is working really well?

Chapter 20

Star Nurseries

....

In the short Old Testament prophecy of Joel, the writer forecasts a day when the Lord will pour out His Spirit upon all people. In the New Testament, the Apostle Peter refers to this prophecy when explaining the unique outpouring of the Holy Spirit on the day of Pentecost (Acts chapter 2).

What Joel wrote is that in the future, it would not just be chosen prophets through whom God spoke forth His Word. Instead, all people would be included in this mystery, men and women alike, even those in the low earthly role of servants. Indeed, he predicted that sons and daughters would prophesy. Young men would see visions. And I especially like his statement about old men dreaming dreams.

In the year 2015 I will be an old man of 79, if God allows me to live that long. By August of 2025 I may even have the privilege of celebrating 89 years on this earth. I mention those dates because it is in the second quarter of the 21st century that I expect old eyes like mine to begin seeing huge changes for the good in our churches. By then I envision millions of Christians around the world regularly contributing their input into what happens Sunday after Sunday. No longer content to say, "There's little we can do about sermons or church services," they will have come of age in regard to changing for the better many particulars in the congregations where they worship. Acting in a truly Christian manner, they will not only have learned how to play a critical part in improving what occurs in their own local setting, they will be networking with believers across the country and around the world to ensure that a healthy percentage of the general public doesn't miss out on what is now happening on weekends in the Lord's House. I trust that what is going on can rightly be called another great revival of Christianity.

Viv- words are life-related. "Vivid" means "full of life." A vivacious person has a lively temperament. The prefix *re-* means "again.' So *re-viv* is "again life," or "life coming back again." The suffix *-al* is "regarding or that which pertains to." Thus, *revival* is simply "that which pertains to life coming back again." What I want you to do is envision yourself as playing an early role in a growing movement that, in its time, becomes a groundswell resulting in nothing less than a powerful revival in the church.

I foresee Christians going to church on Sunday, eagerly anticipating they will hear a word from the Lord that will sustain, nurture and support them the rest of the week. It will be as though Christ appeared in the worship space for all eyes to behold, and nothing was as important as being in His Presence. I picture Christians approaching friends, coworkers, neighbors and extended family with the invitation, "Please come with me to church for worship. The most amazing things happen. I can't really explain it; you have to experience it for yourself." This vision includes wholehearted service-participation on the part of all the listeners because they expect the Holy Spirit to convict them of sin, instruct them as to righteous living, or comfort them when they are sorrowing.

This future revival, this life coming back to God's people, includes weeks where they remember what their worship was about and the words their preacher spoke. They will mull over and over the meaning of Sunday, and find time in their daily lives to make any changes that were put on their hearts. I envision a time in America when Christians are distinctly different from non-churchgoers, not so much in what they don't do but in what they do. They care about the poor. They are good neighbors. They sacrifice their abundance for the sake of the underprivileged. They serve church and community. They find deep joy in the midst of sorrow. Their marriage covenant is a bond that keeps them growing together as couples. They refuse job advantages that will prohibit them from being good parents. They include the outcast in their social events. They are deeply concerned about holiness, and they look forward to attendance in God's house because the spiritual meaning they experience there embraces all of their living. Indeed, Sundays, when God's people gather in churches all over the land, are the high point of their weeks.

Let's make known that right now, this pregnant moment, is the time for members and regular attenders to start graciously offering ministers their thoughts regarding the blockbuster church event of each week—the pastor's sermon plus the service elements that surround it. This critical hour, or whatever the length of your worship service, is designed to help participants both attribute worth to God (worship) and learn how to become more like His Son. Restated, you should be aware of personally praising God along with the rest of the congregation for what you know Him to be. You should also be reminded of what it means to be His son or daughter and challenged to live accordingly.

What then is your great expertise in this new vision? It's nothing more complicated than the following: You alone know whether these goals are being met in your life. Are you conscious of worshiping the Lord when you gather with His people? If not, why not? Are you becoming more Christ-like as you progress in years? If you're not maturing spiritually, why aren't you? These are personal questions only you can answer. Your spiritual-growth quotient, its exciting progress or the fact that it is at a stalemate, needs be shared, if churches are ever to know the better future we all desire.

Before starting this book, you might have said, "I don't know how to do that!" Hey, I realize my help hasn't prepared you to teach a semester-long course on "Effective Preaching Techniques." That wasn't my intent anyway. But certainly by now, you ought to be better at figuring out the subject (question one) of your pastor's sermons each Sunday. And if you aren't, you need to figure out why not!

No great intelligence or exceptional listening skills should be required to catch the response (question two) being called for in such messages either. If the challenge is not clear, the problem needs to be lovingly confronted.

Do the sermons you hear help you with specific how-tos (question 3) in areas where you are struggling? Have you let your pastor know what those difficulties are? In churches where confession is practiced, the clergy have a feeling for what's tripping up their people in the spiritual-progress path. From the sermons I hear in some settings, I get the impression the speaker doesn't believe anyone in the congregation has trouble with jealousy, anger, profanity, lust, pride, lying, wasting time (sloth) or other similar sins. The Christian life is really not all that complicated. God didn't design it exclusively for intellectuals. (Although theology certainly can be intellectually challenging—don't think Christianity is a faith just for dummies, either.) If the sermons you hear aren't helping you to live out your faith, then you need to say so. "Pastor, I'm having trouble getting from A to B, and I need you to be more specific about how to do that!"

Spiritually speaking, are you a quick learner, or do you need a little more time to get it? And how can you tell if you have no idea what is the norm? For instance, are there measurable milestones that can be pointed out regarding the matter of proficiency in prayer? What's the timeline for becoming a holy person? That's why I've included "how long" (question 4) as the last point to consider.

As regards the church (and its effect on your personal desire to be Christ-like) you must believe that you have the ability and the opportunity to change things for the better. No, you don't have a degree in religious studies, but your layperson expertise includes knowing when something works for you and when it doesn't. When it's not working, you now have enough direction to at least initiate the process of change.

If you still feel inept at communicating where you are spiritually, at least you have this book. Why not ask your pastor to read and discuss it with you?

You don't have to be content just to usher. Help usher in the new day! Don't just run the sound system; help make sure the words and music are understandable and vital. Be one of the many men and women, sons and daughters, young folk and old, through whom God speaks in this era when His Spirit rests on all people. If Jesus hinted to fishermen, "You'll do just fine following me," can He not imply the same today to farmers, factory workers, and fashion designers?

Then when your church creates something really good, be sure to put it into a written form that can be shared with other congregations. Every weekend, hundreds of thousands of church services are held in the United States alone. Even if just one in a thousand included a sermon of exceptional value, or a service part that was creative, different and full of meaning, that would still result in hundreds of fresh concepts being generated each week. Multiply that by 52 weeks a year and you come face-to-face with the reality that 15-20,000 marvelous new ideas are being spawned annually. And that number is just a fraction of what is taking place. All kinds of congregations today are wrestling with the question of how to make their sermons and services more meaningful.

I am surprised, though, at the amount of great work that never finds life beyond its initial presentation. With the incredible communication tools available to us, all kinds of networking should be going on between creators of church dramas, music, videos, poems, banners, Scripture readings, you name it, including sermons. Yes, some resources measure up to professional standards and the creators may be justified in charging fees for what they offer. But many are the efforts of volunteers who would be more than pleased to give away what they've created for the sake of the whole Body of Christ.

So treasure the connections you make with people who share your passion for (say) illustrated children's sermons. Send your best work to such soul-mates. Receive theirs in return. Expand your circle of acquaintances concerned about revitalizing worship, and by so doing, prepare for your unique participation in the great revival that can't be far off.

The Chandra X-ray Observatory was named after Subrahmanyan Chandrasekhar. In 1999, four years after his death, when it was launched in the Space Shuttle *Columbia*, it was the latest state-of-the-art x-ray telescope. Appropriately, its mission was to seek out black holes in outer space. The Chandra Observatory not only cleared up numerous previously unsolvable mysteries that eluded astronomers and astrophysicists for years, it was a fantastic witness to all sorts of extraordinary cosmic events.

Not being literate in physics, let me try to reduce this event to language *I* can understand. One of the more intriguing stellar mysteries was a mysterious source of x-rays in the center of a galaxy named NGC 6240. To remind you of the vast immensities astronomers deal with, the gallery is in the constellation Ophiuchus, which is, according to Arthur Miller in *Empire of the Stars*, "2,400 million trillion miles away (that is 25 trillion times the distance from Earth to the Sun)." Due to the speed at which light travels, we are seeing NGC 6240 as it was 400 million years ago. Previous x-ray observatories were a combination of radio, optical and infrared detectors. The Chandra X-ray Observatory, however, had advanced super-sharp resolutions and was able to identify that NGC 6240 is the product of two galaxies colliding, each with its own active black hole.

Astronomers term this a "starburst galaxy," actually a star nursery in which new stars are birthing, then evolving, and sometimes exploding in the aftermath of a galaxy merger estimated to have occurred 30 million years ago.

If you will allow this old man his visions, I see this as an apt metaphor for the "collision" merging the gifts of the pulpit and the pew. I believe the Lord of light and life would love for clergy and laity to labor together in a way that the force of the black holes that once sucked up meaning is now utilized to birth wonderful new bursts of communicative "star light." I would love to believe that all the work that goes into creating Sunday sermons and services (those tens of thousands of creative ideas spun out annually from congregations across the country) would be a "star nursery" in which the reality of the life of Christ captures the imagination of Christians worldwide, creating ripples in the fabric of earth time that spins forward into eternal time.

As night draws closer, the dream of this aging Christian is of an evening sky filled with dancing lights everywhere he looks. I'm told there are more heavenly bodies the size of our earth or larger than there are grains of sand upon the face of the earth. That's an amazing truth.

Scripture declares that the One who spangled the universe with all this luminescence is also the Head of the Church. So I would ordinarily be reluctant to write a whole book about black holes that suck up sermons if I didn't believe my words could play a role in eventually making it appear that the stars shone all the brighter. The Psalmist wrote,

"The heavens declare the glory of God, and the skies proclaim the work of his hands." In the New Testament, the Apostle Paul assigns this task additionally to all believers who are *"to shine like stars in the universe"* (Philippians 2:13).

The truth is, that's what times of authentic revival are like. Such eras involve all parts of the church reflecting the glory of Christ. Yes, ordained clergy are very important. But these are days when ministers desperately need the help of those who usually just listen to them. Pastors need men and women, sons and daughters, who will love them even as the One who called them to His service does. They need parishioners with whom they can form bonds of trust. Most of all, preachers need to know what's happening in the lives of these people as a result of their sermons.

This old man believes that hearing your loving and honest response to their preaching will enable your spiritual leaders to direct you to that new day for which all of us pray. Then like ancient Simeon in Luke 2:29, this white-haired steward will be able to thankfully say to his Lord, "My eyes have seen what I longed for. Now You can dismiss Your servant in peace."

One Last Thought

Say you were to invest 15 to 20 hours every week preparing a meal for the same group of 100 or so people. As they leave these times together, a few say "thank you," but not all that many. True, they contribute toward the expenses of what's served, and you are compensated for your time, but hardly anyone talks about the effort you put forth. Worse yet, it's just hours before they seem to have little or no recall about what it was you served.

My guess is that would discourage you.

Throughout this book, you as a layperson have probably sensed that I have been quite gentle in the way I have written about pastors.

That's because I have personally heard many of them share their pain and frustration.

This is not to imply that none who fill the clergy ranks are egotistical, or sharp-tongued, or control freaks, or narcissists, or crybabies. It's just that whatever else they are, I also know that many of them long for affirmation, especially about their sermons. But this is not something they get much of.

A large number of preachers I know feel their efforts are both inadequate and unappreciated. But their job description means they need to begin almost immediately working on next Sunday's spiritual meal, even though not a lot of those who were served the previous Sunday seemed to care that much for what was put before them.

My desire has been to suggest a workable solution that truly honors all parties involved.

About the Author

David R. Mains Planted a church in the heart of Chicago to reverse church flight from the inner city (1967-1977). Pioneered meaningful worship for contemporary believers, the integration of the arts, and the use of lay gifts.

Established a racially integrated staff and congregation and elevated the role of women.

Experimented with practical response tools for measurable growth, Launched Step 2 to train pastors in renewal principles nationally. Became director of the national radio broadcast *The Chapel of the Air* and immediately designed programs to support the local church (1977-1998). Received an honorary doctorate from Indiana Wesleyan University for his role in contributing to the life of the national church.

Began 50-Day Spiritual Adventures as a way to link religious media to the local church and to the local religious radio outlet. Established the daily national television show *You Need to Know* and won Programmer of the Year Award from National Religious Broadcasters in 1995. Formed Mainstay Church Resources to provide spiritual growth tools for the local church, which eventually was used by 15,000 churches and millions of laypeople.

Created the Advent Celebration, a Christmas series for busy pastors. Developed the Mainstay Model, a sermon preparation tool to radically transform the effectiveness of preaching. Created www. Sermon-Coach.com, a sermon and worship service Web site to provide tools for local pastors.

Why has this man given his life to serving the local church? And why is he concentrating these last decades on mentoring pastors?

David R. Mains believes that a local church, aware of the living presence of Christ, where staff and lay believers work productively together, can radically alter the trajectory of society.

We think that out of the rich years of failures and successes, of seeing God bless and of enduring his silence, he has something to give to you. We invite you to take advantage of this rare opportunity.